Pan Breakthrough Books

KW-484-976

Pan Breakthrough Books open the door to successful self-education. The series provides essential knowledge using the most modern self-study techniques.

Expert authors have produced clear explanatory texts on business subjects to meet the particular needs of people at work and of those studying for relevant examinations.

A highly effective learning pattern, enabling readers to measure progress step-by-step, has been devised for Breakthrough Books by the National Extension College, Britain's leading specialists in home study.

Chris Brewster is an industrial relations consultant, teacher and journalist, based in Cambridge. He acquired varied insights into industrial relations, working for the AUEW, the Commission on Industrial Relations and in the construction and air transport industries before a spell at Kingston Regional Management Centre.

Chris Brewster is co-author of Industrial Relations Training for Managers.

Pan Breakthrough Books

Other books in the series

Background to Business
The Business of Communicating:
    Improving Communication Skills
The Business of Data Processing
Keep Account:
    A Guide to Profitable Bookkeeping
Making Numbers Work:
    An Introduction to Business Numeracy
Management: A Fresh Approach
Marketing: A Fresh Approach
Practical Accounts 1
Practical Business Law
Practical Company Law
Practical Cost and Management
    Accounting
Understanding Office Practice
Using Statistics in Business 1
Using Statistics in Business 2
What Do You Mean 'Communication'?
    An Introduction to Communication in
    Business

Pan Breakthrough Books

Understanding Industrial Relations

Chris Brewster

A Pan Original
Pan Books, London and Sydney

If you wish to study the subject matter of this book in more depth, write to the National Extension College, 18 Brooklands Avenue, Cambridge CB2 2HN, for a free copy of the Breakthrough Business Courses leaflet. This gives details of the extra exercises and professional postal tuition which are available.

First published 1984 by Pan Books Ltd,
Cavaye Place, London SW10 9PG
© Chris Brewster 1984
ISBN 0 330 28221 2

Photoset by Parker Typesetting Service, Leicester
Printed in Great Britain by
Richard Clay (The Chaucer Press) Ltd,
Bungay, Suffolk

Acknowledgements

It would be impossible to acknowledge all the help I have had in writing this book. I learnt a lot from the great number of managers and union officials who have taken part in the training programmes I have run. I would like to thank a few people by name: Roger Oldcorn, who got me started; and two colleagues from Employment Relations Ltd, Anni Hollings, who was always ready to help me improve the text, and Janet Sellwood, who kept me organised. My thanks also go to Lynn and Rebecca, who kept it all in perspective.

Contents

	Preface	9
1	What are industrial relations?	11
2	Management	34
3	The trade unions	53
4	Industrial relations and the state	76
5	The law and collective bargaining	97
6	Individuals and employment law	113
7	Workplace industrial relations	139
8	Negotiating	161
9	Management policies	194
	Further reading	212
	Glossary of terms	214
	Index	221

Preface

There can be few subjects which receive as much attention as industrial relations. It is constantly in the newspapers and on television; it is the source of countless pub discussions. Yet for many of us our knowledge about industrial relations is somewhat scanty.

Often this may not matter too much – lack of knowledge rarely prevents people having an opinion! For two groups, however, such ignorance can be crucial: *Understanding Industrial Relations* provides some basic facts and raises some of the central issues specifically for these groups.

There are, first, managers – in industry, in commerce, in the public and private sectors, in large and small organisations. A central part of their task involves managing their relationships with their subordinates, though often they have little training in or experience of industrial relations.

Second, there are those who are about to face up to industrial relations in the UK: students who are completing their courses and hoping to get a job, people moving into jobs with greater industrial relations responsibilities and managers from abroad coming to this country for the first time. This book will help them all to understand industrial relations.

It is of course a contentious and value-laden subject. That is what makes it so fascinating. Facts about industrial relations may be neutral but the way they are presented can vary. I have set out to challenge opinions – not to get you to change your mind, but to make you clearer about the basis of your opinion. In order to do so I have tried to make the book easy to read and to convey the excitement of the subject. Perhaps where it falls short of these targets you could take it as a challenge!

Whilst I have tried to write simply and clearly I have tried to remain analytical. This is not a schoolboy text. It requires, at least, an intelligent appreciation of the daily news and, at best, experience within employing organisations.

The first chapter of the book examines the subject of industrial relations in general, and the next three consider the main parties involved: the management, the unions and the state. Chapters 5 and 6 examine the legal framework, and the following three chapters examine industrial relations practice in employing organisations.

1 | What are industrial relations?

Industrial relations are an important feature of modern life, yet there is no generally agreed definition of what they are. The purpose of this chapter is to show why that is the case. But it should also enable you to explain the definition of industrial relations that we will be using, if only by implication, throughout the book.

Here are some extracts from recent newspaper reports:

1 Printing workers on *The Times* have agreed to call off their threatened strike following an intervention by the conciliation service ACAS. A spokesman for the print workers claimed that management had withdrawn its insistence on the operation of new printing machinery.

2 Another 2000 workers in the steel industry are to lose their jobs under the latest stage of plans to make the industry viable.

3 The government intends to make union leaders more responsive to their members. Introducing a discussion paper which could lead to further restrictions on trade unions the Employment Secretary launched an attack on 'undemocratic' union leaders. The response from the TUC was predictably frosty.

4 Workers at Heathrow Airport run a serious risk of injury or even death according to members of a local safety committee. 'If passengers knew the size and weight of the cargo we have to move, commented one member, 'they would get out of the plane and give us a hand.'

5 Auditors at the Clapham offices of one of Britain's major unions have discounted claims of malpractice. 'Everything has been carried out and recorded in accordance with normal book-keeping practice', they reported.

Self-check

Which of the above extracts are about 'industrial relations'? Write down the numbers on a piece of paper. Can
you think of some words, to describe the extracts you
would not call industrial relations?

ANSWER

There is no right answer – or rather there are several right
answers. One of the most important things to bear in mind in any
discussion about industrial relations is that they are a value-laden
and disputed subject. Everything that is said or written about
them (and you must include this book) is based on a range of
assumptions about fundamental issues of what is right, what is
fair and what is reasonable. The values that we each hold – and
the muddled and contradictory form that they can take – will
have a major impact on our view of the subject.

Fact or opinion?

There is very little in industrial relations that we can describe as a
fact, much of it that is value-laden opinion. This is central to all
discussions of the subject, though it is rarely recognised (or
perhaps often forgotten) by those who discuss it. As we go
through this book we shall find that even basic 'facts' (such as the
number of trade unions) are open to dispute. We should not be
surprised therefore if the problems that some people discuss are
not accepted as problems by others; or, if they are, that the
solutions proposed are significantly varied.

This potential and real variety of views and their relationship
to fundamental beliefs help make industrial relations so fascinating. They can also make the subject very frustrating. How
can we study a subject with no right answers?

Well, in the same way that we can study music. The picture is
not all confused: there are basic patterns, there are 'highs' and
'lows', there are different styles. And studies can be more or less
sophisticated, whilst retaining the element of personal preference.

Self-check

Let's look back at our first question. How do we find the correct definition of industrial relations so that we can decide which of the extracts from the press on p. 11 should be included in it?

ANSWER

We realise that there is *no* 'correct' definition. Different definitions are available, and are used in everyday situations. You must have had some underlying definition in mind when you first assessed the five extracts.

Did your definition have something to do with trade unions? Most of us would include them in industrial relations. So we would include reports numbers 1 and 3. What about number 5? It is certainly a trade union; some of you will therefore have classified it as an industrial relations story. Others will have wanted to exclude it; it is about a union but not about anything the unions *do*. It is an internal matter of the kind that could apply to a cricket club or a small shop. It could just as easily be characterised as an accounts item, or perhaps as business or organisation.

Item number 4 does not mention unions at all. Still, many readers might have wanted to include such stories under industrial relations. If you have included this one you would perhaps argue that industrial relations are about more than just trade unions. They are about people at work and the terms and conditions under which they are employed.

This is a wider definition. It would encompass newspaper items numbers 1, 3 and 4 but not 5 and perhaps not 2. The extract about job losses in the steel industry could be seen as 'economic'.

One definition

There are even wider definitions which would encompass all five extracts. Industrial relations can be defined as being about:

the relationship between workers and their organisations, managers and their organisations and governmental agencies concerned with the workplace and employment generally.

On this definition the closure of a steelworks, which will affect the relationship between the steel company and the steel unions, is very much an industrial relations issue.

It has been argued that we should exclude from this definition all *individual* items and only include in our discussion of industrial relations those items which are resolved *collectively* or, in other words, by *groups* of workers or the unions that represent such groups. After all, it might be argued, pay scales and arrangements for handling disputes are what industrial relations are all about; but individual work schedules, or foremen discussing last night's football with the workers, are not. These single-person items, it could be said, are matters of personnel management.

Let us, at least at this stage, take the definition set out on p. 13 as a workable basis for getting into the subject.

Self-check

How many of the following events are included in industrial relations on that definition?

1 A wage negotiation.
2 A complaint that a worker is not being paid enough, made to the foreman.
3 A complaint that shift pay has been miscalculated, made to the wife.
4 A debate at a union branch meeting about unilateral nuclear disarmament.
5 A debate at a union branch meeting about shift work patterns.
6 A management meeting about buying new lorries.
7 A management meeting about new disciplinary rules.
8 A management meeting about providing a quicker service to customers.
9 A visit to the building site by a health and safety inspector.
10 A government scheme to give young black school-leavers a chance to work for three months in a factory.

ANSWER

Even on our working definition it is a matter of degree. Some of these (**1, 2, 5, 7, 9, 10**) fit easily into it. A complaint made to the wife (**3**) is not industrial relations because it doesn't include management or government; but if the employee raises it with his boss in the morning it will fit our definition. And it might fit our definition if he does not raise it, but harbours a grudge – that may well affect the relationship with his boss indirectly. CND debates at union branch meetings (**4**) will not affect the management, but they might if the union members started collecting signatures on a petition during working hours, for example.

What about **6** and **8**? It is more difficult to disentangle the management involvement in industrial relations because nearly everything that management does affects the relationship with the workforce. In general not much of a manager's time is spent taking decisions about the workforce directly; it is just that the workforce is involved in nearly all of the manager's other decisions. For instance, choosing a new lorry (**6**) is a financial and operational decision, but it will have a very real effect on the work and response of the lorry drivers. A quicker service to customers (**8**) may be a marketing decision, but it may put more pressure on the staff and will affect their relationships with their boss.

It may be easiest to see industrial relations as a circle with blurred edges. In the centre are the unions and management in negotiation. Other factors, such as decisions about purchasing new equipment, are on the edge – they are part of it but also part of other subject circles. Sometimes, however, these issues at the margin will end up in the centre.

Activity

Think of five things that an organisation (perhaps the one you work in, or one you know of) does. Draw a circle to represent 'industrial relations' and then place these other activities in relation to industrial relations – inside the circle, at the centre; on the edge; or outside it, far away and having no impact.

Work in Britain

The subject of industrial relations is about people at work. Nearly all males and about half the females between school-leaving and retirement ages go to work – or, sadly, want to go to work but cannot find any. In Britain this mean that some twenty-two million people are at work.

Most of them work for someone else. They do not own their own businesses and employ others; less than 3 per cent do that. Nor do they work for themselves, employing only their own labour; only 7 per cent do that.

Those who employ others, as well as those who are employed, are actors on the industrial relations stage. Roughly one in ten of those who are employed work in managerial roles. They fall into both the managerial and the employee categories and have a particularly complicated position in industrial relations.

This is where the definitions begin to show their effect. If you had defined industrial relations as just being about trade unions, for example, there would be lots of people at work who were not involved in them. On our definition those who are not in trade unions are included.

Self-check

What about the self-employed, working only for themselves? Can you think of any way in which a self-employed painter might be involved in industrial relations?

ANSWER

History is littered with cases of self-employed people causing industrial relations disputes. Workers at a factory might claim that a self-employed painter is putting one of the regular factory-employed painters out of work; or they might be annoyed by the extra money he is being paid for the painting contract (or by how cheaply he is expected to work). There does not have to be a dispute for his employment to affect the relationship between managers and employees at the factory. Once it does affect that relationship, in any way, we can argue that even the self-employed worker is involved in industrial relations.

Normally, however, we will be using the term to refer to people at work and the relationships between employees and their employers or managers. Clearly the nature and form of work are important. We will also be including relationships which are *about* that relationship but may not be *at* work – between managers and trade unions for example, or between trade unions and government agencies concerned with work.

Activity

Which of the following jobs and occupations are directly involved in industrial relations, which might be, and which could not be?

1 A lorry driver employed by a petrol company.
2 A mother at home.
3 A nurse.
4 A freelance film producer.
5 A lorry driver who owns his own lorry.
6 A monk.
7 A computer programmer employed by a university.
8 A trade union official.
9 A marketing director of a food company.
10 A Member of Parliament.

ANSWER

Well, let's check who is involved at work in relationships between managers and employees (and their respective organisations) and perhaps government agencies concerned with work. Directly involved will be the lorry driver (1), the nurse (3) and computer programmer (7), as employees. The trade union official (8), as a representative of employees (and as an employee of his own union) is also directly involved. So are the film producer (4) and the marketing director (9), as employer or manager. The mother (2) and the monk (6) may work very hard but they are not 'at work' in our terms. The self-employed lorry driver may or may not be, as we have said. As for the Member of Parliament, it depends on whether he decides to act in this area or not.

Of course none of these people, not even the trade union official, is involved in industrial relations all the time they are at work. Even trade union officials will sometimes drink coffee or dream of a win on the football pools. For most people in employment, though, major aspects of their working lives will be conditioned by industrial relations.

The contract of employment

So industrial relations are involved in all employment. But what impact do they have on individuals in employment? The most obvious impact is on the terms and conditions under which the employee works. Despite all the strictures of economists and other commentators it is still the case that how much an individual is paid, what they have to do for it and the circumstances in which they work are all decided between employers or managers and employees or their representatives.

In practice individual employees rarely get the chance to agree the basic terms of the relationship between themselves and their boss. More typically wage rates, hours of work and the sort of work expected are decided by negotiation with a trade union or by the updating of historical tradition. The employee agrees merely to join the organisation on those terms and conditions, or to stay in employment.

There are also, of course, a range of ways in which employees and managers are connected which fall outside the formal written terms of the contract of employment.

Activity

Write down three subjects on which an employee may communicate with his or her boss which fall outside the written terms of the contract.

ANSWER

The potential relationship beyond the formal terms is vast. You may have restricted yourself to matters close to the work: discussions about a way of improving the work flow that the employee has devised, or about the organisation of the job. You may have thought wider: to discussions about other departments or customers. You may have thought of some communication which had absolutely nothing to do with the work: last night's television or some amorous liaison!

All of these, to the extent that they affect the relationship with the boss, are grist to our mill. Naturally, the more tangible issues, those normally included in the written contract terms, are central to our interest; the others will become more peripheral as they become more individual and have less impact on the relationship between employee and manager. Often the more tangible issues will involve the trade unions, but they need not.

We are now in a position to improve our picture of industrial relations. The fuzzy circle that we had – activity, p. 15 – can be redrawn as a series of circles, with the contract of employment at the centre. Look at your own diagram again and see if you can visualise it that way. My diagram looks like this:

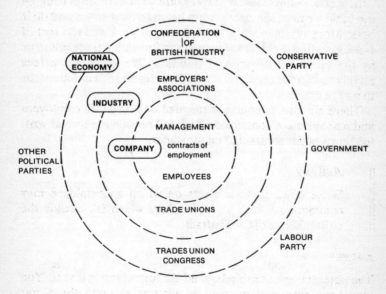

Figure 1.

Activity

Can you transfer from your initial diagram on to my diagram the things that your organisation does? You will need to bear in mind that events can move particular subjects into the centre on some occasions and out to the edge on others. If you cannot fit your items on to my diagram you may have to think about amending it.

Are industrial relations important?

Activity

Look through today's newspaper. How many of the stories in it are concerned with industrial relations?

ANSWER

There may be days when not a single one of the stories in the newspaper or on the main television news are concerned with industrial relations. These days are very rare, however Mostly there will be several stories which are concerned with industrial relations; and on some days there seems to be almost nothing else.

This amount of attention is not paid to other subjects (nor, incidentally, does the press in other countries pay so much attention to industrial relations). Indeed, not many other topics have so many books written about them either! We should try to understand at the outset why industrial relations are seen as so important.

The answer to this question can be given in four parts. Industrial relations are important because:

- Work is such a central activity for most adults.
- Everyone is affected by industrial relations.
- Bad industrial relations can damage our economy.
- Good industrial relations give potential and far-reaching benefits.

Work as a central activity

We have already seen that most adult males and about half the adult females are working (or are unemployed but would like to be working).

Activity

Think of three ways in which work is important to an individual.

ANSWER

You would have found it harder to think of three ways in which it was unimportant! Work dominates time: an individual may spend up to half a normal working day in getting ready for work, travelling there, being at work, journeying home. Most of us spend more of our waking hours at work than everywhere else put together, at least on a working day.

Work affects our social life. How much money we have to spend, whom we know, how other people regard us, how we are expected to behave – in short, how we live is determined by our work. In a slightly different sense work will have an impact on how happy we are, what our health is like and perhaps on our leisure activities, who our friends are or where we live.

So work is vital to us. That means, in turn, that industrial relations are important.

Activity

Look at the aspects we have discussed in thinking about work, listed below. How many of those are (a) affected by relationships between employees and managers, or even (b) subject to agreements between trade unions and managers? Mark the items (a), (b) or 'not'. We discussed:

1 Time at work.
2 How much money we have.
3 Whom we know.
4 How other people regard us.

   5 How we are expected to behave.
   6 How happy we are.
   7 The state of our health.
   8 Our leisure activities.
   9 Who our friends are.
  10 Where we live.

ANSWER

It is possible to argue that all these aspects are affected to a greater or lesser extent by the way that you, for example, get on with your boss. It is equally possible to argue that for most of us factors outside the workplace play a very important part in all of these. How many of these aspects are affected by union – management agreements will vary. Typically the agreements would have a major impact on how much time we spend at work (**1**), how much we get for it (**2**), how we are expected to behave, at least at work (**5**), and our health and safety (**7**), and perhaps where the work is located – hence where we live (**10**). The agreements may also have some effect on how other people regard us (**4**) and how happy we are (**6**) will depend to some extent on the results of the union – management negotiation.

   For most people work is a central factor in their lives; industrial relations are a central factor in their work.

The impact of industrial relations

As industrial relations are so central to the work context, they will have an impact on every household where anyone works. The effect goes much further than that, though, because industrial relations will affect not only those directly involved, but all of us as well.

   Suppose that a major engineering factory and the nearby office of a building society both suffer from poor industrial relations. In the factory this will take the form of antagonism between the union representatives and the management as well as between individual employees and managers. In the building society office it will just result in strained relations between, say, the counter staff and the manager.

What are the impacts on you and me? Well, industrial action such as go-slows or bans on overtime working in the factory may mean that we cannot buy the goods we want when we want them. In the building society office we may find that the staff are less helpful than usual, or make mistakes in our account.

Nor do the workplace where industrial relations are poor have to be located near us. The factory may supply goods all over the country. It may be at the building society's head office two hundred miles away that some aggrieved employee fails to pay proper attention to your account.

Industrial relations affect us all in these undramatic ways. They can also have a much more general and visible impact. A strike on the railways affects millions. Industrial action by teachers will have an impact wherever there are schoolchildren, and may have a consequent impact on many other workplaces if parents have to stay at home. A dispute in the banks will give nearly everyone problems.

This widespread effect is one of the reasons why the press and television pay such detailed attention to industrial relations.

Activity

Take an industrial dispute that you have recently seen mentioned on television or in the newspapers. Can you think of any potential ways in which it could affect you?

Economic impact of bad industrial relations

The effect of industrial relations problems is not just felt in individual, or even mass, inconvenience. These problems also have a significant economic result. Bad industrial relations make organisations less able to fulfil their overall objectives. Let us take some examples.

Activity

What is the key objective of the following organisations? (Just one objective for each.)

● A supermarket.

- A hospital.
- A building company.
- A water works.
- A hotel.

Each organisation will have a range of objectives. Many of them will be important. For three of these organisations, however, we can identify a key objective of profit: key in the sense that, if they do not make profits, they will cease to exist. These three are the supermarket, the building company and the hotel. The hospital and the water works are different: they have an objective of providing particular services.

With poor industrial relations, these objectives are in danger. Aggrieved employees will work less well, may refuse certain work or may cease to work altogether by leaving that employment or going on strike. The effect will be to threaten profits or to restrict or curtail the service. This will create difficulties for the organisation. If such a situation becomes widespread in different organisations, it will weaken the economy of the country as a whole.

We can get a preliminary idea of the extent of this problem by looking at its most obvious feature: strikes.

Self-check

Would you say that in the UK there are:

- a lot of strikes?
- quite a large number of strikes?
- a moderate amount of strikes?
- not many strikes?

There are, generally, something over 2000 strikes reported in the UK per year. In an average year, they occur in only 2 per cent of establishments. Even in the manufacturing industries, which attract a lot of newspaper coverage, over 90 per cent of workplaces have no strikes in an average year. Whether you think that is a lot, quite a lot, moderate or not many is a matter of individual judgement.

Table 1. Working days lost per 1000 employees through industrial disputes, EEC countries – all industries and services

Country	Average for ten years 1969–78
UK	472
Belgium	255
Denmark	255
France	205
West Germany	36
Ireland	731
Italy	1460
Netherlands	36

Table 2. Working days lost through industrial disputes per 1000 employees (mining, manufacturing, construction and transport)

Countries	Average for ten years 1969–78
UK	897
Australia	1242
Belgium	467
Canada	1929
Denmark	575
France	297
West Germany	90
India	1379
Ireland	991
Italy	1938
Japan	231
Netherlands	75
Spain	928
United States	1362

It is worth comparing the number of days lost through strikes with the number of days lost through sickness. In the 1970s, when strikes had caused more working days to be lost than at any time since the Second World War, ten million working days were lost through industrial disputes in the average year. In the same period, 350 million days were lost through sickness. It has consequently been suggested that a cure for the common cold would have more impact on industrial productivity than ending all strikes.

How does the UK stand compared to other countries? Look at tables 1 and 2. They show that, in the UK during the ten years up to and including 1978, 472 days were lost per 1000 employees due to strikes. In other words, for every 1000 workers in employment (with each working approximately 240 days) a total amongst all of them of 472 days was spent on strike.

The tables show that Britain is about the middle of the league. There are approximately as many countries with better strike records as there are with worse. The British pattern is, however, different from some others in two respects. First, 95 per cent of strikes in the UK are 'unofficial' – they are decided upon and carried out at the local level and not formally approved by the trade union's regional or national executives. (We will refer to this again in the chapter on trade unions.)

Second, strikes have traditionally been concentrated in a few industries (coalmining, docks, motor vehicle manufacture, shipbuilding, and iron and steel). Recently, however, this concentration is declining as those industries become less strike-prone and others take up the strike weapon.

The potential benefits of good industrial relations

The other side of the coin is rarely stressed, but is just as valid. Poor industrial relations are a cause of distress for those involved and a source of inconvenience for others, as well as being an economic problem for organisations and the country as a whole. Equally, good industrial relations will have a positive impact: work will be more enjoyable, service or profit will be better and there will be a gain for the national economy.

The question this raises is why industrial relations are good in some situations and less good in others. If you know the answer you can make millions, as a consultant! Industrial relations, as we have seen, have many implications and many overlaps with other areas of work and management. The causes of good and bad relationships will inevitably be complex and difficult to discover.

Part of the cause, the explanation for industrial relations, lies in the actions of management. Industrial relations are affected by the working environment (the industry, size of workplace and occupation). There is considerable evidence that certain industries have better industrial relations records than others, and that better industrial relations are found in smaller workplaces and amongst certain occupations.

Nevertheless, even in similar circumstances some organisations have better industrial relations than others. The obvious explanation for this lies in the way these organisations are managed. Good industrial relations can be achieved where the management consciously plans to have them, integrates industrial relations into its business objectives and gives them a high priority in the operation of the organisation's work.

> *Activity*
>
> Think of an organisation you know. How are industrial relations (on our definition) regarded by the management of that company? Are they planned? Are they part of all major planning in the organisation – or just a problem that may prevent those plans working?

ANSWER

Organisations can manage in a way that generates good industrial relations. (We will come back to this point later in the book.) If managers want to develop good industrial relations they will need to know who is involved and what happens. Read on.

Where work occurs

Our definition of industrial relations could apply at national level, at industry level or at organisational level. It is fairly obvious that the majority of contact between managers and workers goes on *within* organisations. It is in the factories, offices, departments, shops, sites and studios that employees are managed.

When we think about a workplace, the first thing we need to be clear about is who works where. Leaving aside the old joke – 'How many people work here?' 'Oh, about half of them' – we need to discuss the variety of situations in which people are employed. There are four important factors to include in our discussion of who works where. These are not the only ones – we are not covering regional and geographical location, for example – but they are central to industrial relations. The factors are:

- industry, or industrial sector;
- whether private or public organisation;
- size of workplace;
- occupation.

Industry, or industrial sector

People work in a wide range of industries. Some of these are long-established. There must have been some sort of agriculture and some sort of food industry even before we can find them in the historical records. Some are very new, such as petroleum and chemicals.

There has been an overall shift in employment which we can show if we group industries into three categories:

- *primary*, by which is meant extracting a living directly from nature (mining, fishing, agriculture and so on);
- *manufacture*, the making of things, often in (manu)factories (engineering, chemicals, and textiles would be examples);
- *service*, everything else.

These are only broad groupings. Manufacture, for example, will cover everything from the making of horse harnesses to the production of microchips. We do not need government statistics to tell us that within the grouping of manufacture there will have been major changes over the years. Fewer people will be employed making horse harnesses now than fifty years ago, whilst the number of people making microchips is increasing all the time.

Whole industries grow and decline. There is a continuing reduction in the number of people employed in agriculture, mining, railways and steelmaking. There are more employees in computer and video manufacture. Additionally, the balance between the different sectors of work is also changing. Recent decades have seen a growth in the service sector of the British economy at the expense of manufacturing.

> *Activity*
>
> What would be some differences between, say, making gas meters (manufacture) and reading the meters (service)?

ANSWER

To summarise all the differences between a manufacturing job and a service job, you might identify some general points:

- Service jobs tend to be cleaner.
- Manufacturing is often performed among large numbers of workers; service jobs are more often done singly or in small groups.
- Service jobs often involve meeting members of the public; manufacturing jobs rarely do.
- Manufacturing is usually carried out in one immovable location; many service jobs involve the worker moving around geographical areas.

Although to some extent personal preference is involved, most people seem to find service jobs a more pleasant source of work than manufacturing jobs. Service employment has increased in Britain far more than in most other countries. The proportion of non-industrial or service jobs is higher in the UK than in most of our competitor nations.

There has been another very important change. Not only have the service industries in general become comparatively bigger. It is increasingly the case that *public sector* services – those owned by the state – are employing more and more of the labour force.

Private vs public sector

In broad terms, over the last twenty or so years, it is the public service sector of employment which has grown most rapidly. There has been a significant growth in employment in central government (usually referred to as the civil service) and local government, including the health service, education, local authorities, police and so on. This is a controversial trend. It is not that anyone doubts that it is happening, but some people wonder whether it should be happening.

The reducing of employment in manufacturing and the growth in public employment have had a significant impact on the way people work. They have therefore also had a significant impact in industrial relations. We will look again at their effects later on in the book.

Size of workplace

This is the third factor which has a big impact on industrial relations. There are three million enterprises in Britain, ranging in size from a workforce of one to workforces of hundreds of thousands. The larger organisations are often split up amongst a great many geographical locations (you will sometimes see them referred to as 'multi-plant' or 'multi-site').

Take the example of Tube Investments (TI), one of Britain's major manufacturing companies. In fact TI is a group of companies, which includes many household names: the Raleigh bike company, the Swan electric kettle company, Bacofoil and so on – over 100 in all. Some of these companies in turn operate in a number of geographically spread buildings.

Most workplaces are very small. Nearly half of all employees, however, are employed in a small number of large workplaces with over 1000 employees. The range is enormous. I worked for a while with a steeplejack gang high up in the roof of a Sheffield steelworks: a giant place, nearly half a mile long, full of awesome machinery, heat and noise. Below our feet, dwarfed by the surroundings, hundreds of people worked. My next job was in a quiet office, working with seven others. You may not have had the variety of size of workplace brought home to you quite so vividly, but you will need to bear it in mind throughout any discussion of industrial relations.

There has been a continual growth in the size of workplaces throughout this century, but that may now be reversing. First, as the recession has hit companies they have made employees redundant. Often the bigger establishments find it easier to reduce the number of staff they employ. Second, new technological developments mean that people no longer need to work in such large conglomerations: it is getting easier to organise work in smaller units, linked by sophisticated communications systems.

The occupational structure

So far then we have isolated three factors; industrial sector, whether private or public organisation and size of workplace. The fourth one identified was occupation, meaning the type of job being performed. Usually, though not always, employees are classified according to the things that they are expected to do.

In Britain, unlike Japan for instance, people are not employed as a 'company worker', rather they are employed as an electrician, a nurse, a computer programmer, a storesman or whatever. They are not generally expected, and do not expect themselves, to change from doing an electrician's job to a nurse's or from programming to shopkeeping. These expectations are part of the implied terms of the contract of employment – and Parliament has insisted that the occupational title is included in the written particulars of the contract that the employees must be given. Ask a Japanese worker what he does and he will reply, 'I work for Mitsubishi' (or Nissan, etc.); ask a British worker what he does and he will say, 'I am a welder' (or an accountant, etc.).

This reflects traditional work patterns. In Britain employees will change jobs, maybe quite often. They will move from being a salesman in one firm to being a salesman in another, and then perhaps to being a salesman in a totally different industry. But they will stay a salesman. In Japan they will move from being a production worker to a salesman to an office worker – but all with the same company.

In Britain, the differences between occupations have all sorts of connotations attached to them. Being a bricklayer carries with it lots of associations; being a university lecturer carries a quite different set. These implications have permeated our whole way of thought so that often we forget to challenge some of the assumptions. They are part of the British culture, and they are an important part of industrial relations. Many of the trade unions, for example, have established an occupational link. There is one major union for engineers, one for electricians, one for airline pilots, one for musicians, one for health visitors and so on.

Changes in work

The four factors that we have discussed are all subject to *change*. This too is a vital element in industrial relations. We have already seen how some industries have declined and some grown during this century (p. 28). We have also noted the change from private to public sector (p. 29), and changes in size (p. 30).

> *Activity*
>
> Think about the range of occupations. Are the numbers employed in them changing too? Try to think of at least two reasons why they might.

ANSWER

We have already identified some of the reasons why the numbers in each occupation will change. They will do so as the industries change. A small mining industry will mean fewer miners; a growing computer industry will mean more computer designers, computer engineers and programmers and so on. There will also be changes associated with the introduction of new services. A greater emphasis on welfare, for example, has meant that there are now more social workers than ever before. There will be changes too in the way some occupations are carried out. Railway signalmen used to work in isolated 'boxes' up and down railway lines using a lot of muscle-power to pull heavy iron gears. Now they work in groups in well-lit offices monitoring and controlling highly sophisticated computerised signals via a complex visual display. Other occupations are changing just as much.

New technology

Underlying this and many of these changes is the introduction of new technology. This has an extensive impact on work. The technology available to us has changed at an increasing rate throughout history. It has changed almost everything in our world – communications, leisure, home life, war. It has had some of its most dramatic effects at work.

The introduction of new machinery, computer-aided design and manufacture and, in particular, new information technology in the office has created whole new industries and revolutionised existing ones. These changes are continuing. They have affected industries, sectors and occupations. Sooner or later, and in most cases sooner, the new technology will affect every job.

2 | Management

This chapter examines one of the parties to industrial relations – management. By the end of the chapter you should appreciate the key role that management plays in industrial relations. To do that you need to understand the differences within management and the variety of ways that they can be involved, and to have at least a brief acquaintance with the organisations that represent management in industrial relations. We will discuss too the complicated position that managers, who are also employees, find themselves in.

The overall responsibility for industrial relations in Britain is shared between managers, unions and the state agencies involved. The responsibility for industrial relations within the organisation is also shared – but the major responsibility rests with management. It is the management which is responsible for running the organisation, and which should accept responsibility for the industrial relations which are an integral part of that process.

There is a view that the responsibility for bad industrial relations, at least, lies with the trade unions. Certainly when there is an industrial dispute and strikes are called it is the unions' action which is most obvious. But even here the fact that industrial relations in the organisation have reached the point where employees are prepared to stop work must be partly because of management.

Activity

The view that management is mainly responsible for developing and maintaining industrial relations is still a controversial one. Do you agree with it? Try to identify two or three reasons for your agreement or disagreement. Next

time you are with a group of friends find out what they think
– and try to argue the other point of view!

Managers or owners?

Self-check

Our definition of industrial relations (p. 13) refers to
managers and their organisations. Many other definitions of
the subject are more 'logical': in opposition to employ*ees*
they talk about employ*ers* and their organisations. Bearing
in mind the point made on p. 12, that all definitions of
industrial relations are value-laden, why do you think we
specify *managers* rather than employers?

ANSWER

Referring to managers has two main advantages. First, most
organisations do not belong to an employer. The notion of an
'employer' or 'owner of the business' is one that is obviously
useful in explaining the operation of a small business – or a large
business owned by one family (such as Pilkington Glass, or Tesco
or Ford).

But who 'owns' a giant multinational corporation, or a local
authority, or a bank or pension fund, or the Cooperative
Wholesale Society? Who is the 'employer' in such cases? In law a
particular individual – often 'the company secretary' reporting to
the board of directors – can be taken to represent the employer.
But in practice this is an abstraction. Even the local authority's
council, or the bank's board or the CWS executive committee are
in reality representing the local ratepayers, or the shareholders
or the members respectively. They are managing the concern on
behalf of others. Since 'owners' of small companies also 'manage' their concerns, we can use the term 'manager' or 'management' to cover all those who are involved in running
organisations.*

*For a more detailed and yet entertaining discussion about the meaning of the
words 'manager' and 'management' read Roger Oldcorn's book in the Breakthrough series: *Management: A Fresh Approach*.

The second main advantage of referring to 'managers' is that it is closer to the reality of work. It may not be easy to identify who the employer is; but it is far easeir to know who your boss is – and who the other managers in the organisation are. The employer may be an abstraction; but the manager is real – you can bump into him, or annoy him or keep out of his way. And his impact on you will be very apparent.

We should beware, however, of assuming that the interests of managers and owners will be identical.

Activity

Under the two headings of 'managers' and 'owners' write down the likely attitude of each to:

1 Profit.
2 Growth.
3 Maintaining employment.

ANSWER

You might have developed a chart that looks like this:

	Managers	Owners
1 Profit	Sufficient to continue	Maximum
2 Growth	Maximum	Sufficient to yield good profits
3 Maintaining employment	Where possible	Only if profitable

There has been a lot of debate about whether a management can have different interests from the owners of the business. On one side it is argued that ownership is now so widespread and fragmented that it is in fact the managers who control the business (or at least the senior executive managers). On the other side it is argued that owner control still exists, but it is hidden, and/or that managers effectively control the business just as the owners would. This is the result of the common background which senior managers share with owners, the extent to which managers are selected because they share the same beliefs, and the way that they are encouraged to identify themselves with the owners. You must make up your own mind about this debate.

We will be spending more time in this book on the differences of objective between the managers and the employees.

> *Activity*
>
> Under the two headings this time of 'managers' and 'employees' write down the likely attitude of each to:
>
> 1 Wages
> 2 Numbers employed.
> 3 The success of the business.

ANSWER

Your chart this time might look as follows:

	Managers	Employees
1 Wages	Low wages costs	High wages
2 Numbers employed	As few as possible	Security of employment
3 Success of business	Paramount	Important

In short, managers will have interests in common with other employees, and they will also have interests which may be at odds with other employees.

Managerial objectives

On average about one tenth of an organisation's employees may be classified as managerial. What is it that sets this group apart? How do managers differ from other employees?

First, managers have a different job to do. Lord Bertrand Russell once said that there are two kinds of work: the first involves altering the position of matter at or near the surface of the earth; the second involves telling other people to do it. He argued that the key differences were that the second was pleasant and well paid, whilst the first was often neither. This was perhaps a little tongue-in-cheek. The point, however, is accurate. The key tasks of management are deciding on priorities for groups of other people and controlling economic and human resources to achieve those priorities. Other employees do not make such decisions and, whilst they may control economic resources, they do not, or only occasionally, control other people.

Second, managers on the whole have a different background. Management is, as we shall see, enormously varied and so general conclusions such as this have to be treated carefully. Within such a constraint it can be shown that managers (on average at least) have had more education and training and are from a higher social class than the majority of other employees.

Management and industrial relations

The task of management encompasses all the activities of the organisation. Most managers, and most writers on management, quite sensibly see industrial relations, even on our wide definition, as very much a subordinate activity. But think back to the key tasks that management has and consider the importance of industrial relations that we examined in Chapter 1.

Management involves working through other people: getting them to do the work whilst the manager plans, organises, coordinates and controls it. In all these activities most managers are trying to achieve targets: sales, budgets, production, service, time deadlines. Managerial relationships with employees and their representatives are just means to these ends.

They are, of course, crucial means. We saw in Chapter 1 how poor industrial relations could make it impossible for the management to achieve its objectives. Even in a more limited sense the wages and other costs (such as national insurance and pensions) associated with employing staff are the major operating cost for most organisations. If those costs can be kept down, or the work achieved for those costs can be increased, then management will be closer to achieving key objectives of profit or service.

Despite these widely known facts, however, managers still tend to see industrial relations as less important than production, sales or finance. It moves up their priority list only when there is a very obvious problem.

Activity

Why has management accorded industrial relations a low priority? Try to think of at least two reasons.

ANSWER

One reason for this low priority is historical. Looking back through the past, human labour has at most times been readily available, easily replaceable and cheap. Managers could treat staff more or less as they wished knowing that the employees were keen to keep their jobs however unsatisfactory they might be.

A second reason for the low priority managers have accorded industrial relations lies in the fact that many organisations have only recently been unionised. Prior to unionisation employee frustration could only be expressed in individual absenteeism, people leaving or low morale. The economic consequences may be substantial but these individual actions are less 'visible' and obvious to the managers than collective actions such as go-slows or strikes.

Other reasons for the low priority of industrial relations lie in the inadequate training for man management that most managers receive; in the ease of measuring other criteria (such as sales) as against the difficulty of assessing whether industrial relations are good or not; and in the opportunity to pass on the blame (to the shop stewards, employees, or union officials) when things go wrong.

Of course these are generalisations – and managers are all different.

Differences within management

It is in many ways remarkable that managers act in common as much as they do. This is so much a part of our everyday experience that we fail to notice it very often. If you ask the people in your street about some of the local companies they will quite readily tell you that X is a good company to work for, Y is all right but not as good as X and you work in Z only if you're desperate. It doesn't matter whether they are right or not (unless you are offered a job in one). What is significant is that these distinctions can be made even between apparently similar companies in the same industry. What people often mean, and sometimes say, is that management in one organisation treat the employees well, in others not so well.

They have identified sufficient similarity of behaviour amongst a group of very different individuals to be able to classify them all as having a certain management style. This, amongst the very varied individuals (and occasionally eccentric individualists) that make up a management team, is indeed remarkable. We will try to outline in broad terms how this similarity is achieved in a little while, but first let us explore the differences a bit more.

All human beings are individuals and, luckily, unlike any other individual. They can also be looked at as members of groups, and it is by categorising them as groups that we can begin to cope with the infinite variety of people. So we start to think of them as male or female, married or unmarried, or particular nationalities or physical attributes, and in groups which indicate their relationships to other people (husband, father) or their work (doctor, bricklayer).

Activity

Put the following managerial jobs into three groups:

The supervisor in a factory.
The accounts director.
The factory manager in the production department.
The manager of the sales department.
The supervisor of the accounts department's invoice section.
The supervisor in the sales department.
The accounts department manager.
The sales director.
The production director.

ANSWER

You could have done this in one of two ways: by function (the factory/production managers, the sales managers, the accounts managers) or by level (the directors, the departmental managers, the supervisors).

These two differences are sometimes called 'functional' (referring to the variations between departments) and 'hierarchical' (variations between different levels of management). We will deal with them in turn, looking at these differences generally first, and then in relation to industrial relations.

Departmental differences

Most organisations divide employees according to the tasks that they are expected to do. The employees are grouped according to common tasks. Each group is under the direction and control of a manager. In Britain at least it is very common for these managers to come from the occupational group that they are in charge of. The larger the organisation, the more managers there will be in any particular occupational, or as the jargon has it, 'functional' group.

Inevitably, therefore, even in the smallest organisations, we can differentiate between managers according to the functions that they are managing. Typically there may be a production or service manager, a sales manager, an accounts manager, an administration manager; the list is endless. In the largest organisations there may be hundreds of different functional categories. We can, therefore, find numbers of managers in any one organisation who have a similar standing or status but are involved in running totally different parts of the overall operation. This often gives rise to jealousies and conflict.

A company that I know of in West London makes office furniture. The sales managers are not unnaturally keen to sell as much office furniture as they possibly can. One of the ways they can encourage their salesmen to get orders is by allowing them to offer particular tailor-made specifications for different client offices. In this way the number and value of sales are increased and the sales managers are meeting their objectives. The managers in the factory, on the other hand, have different objectives. Their job is to ensure that furniture is produced as cheaply and efficiently and to as high a standard as possible. The best way to do this is to produce long series of identical items. Many management meetings are spent trying to resolve the desire of the sales managers to push tailor-made items and the desire of the production managers to ensure standardisation.

'Line' and 'staff' managers

Not only is there in general a differentiation between functions, and therefore between functional managers; there is increasingly a differentiation made between what are known as 'line' managers and what are known as 'staff' managers. Broadly, a line manager is one who is directly concerned with the organisation and making of products or the provision of the service. Staff managers are those who are responsible for backing up the line manager by providing support in areas such as finance, publicity or, particularly relevant for us, industrial relations. Line managers are all involved in industrial relations. When we come to look at industrial relations policies (in Chapter 9) we will see that they are not only involved, but are central to it. And yet many companies – especially the larger ones – employ specialist industrial relations managers.

They are not always called that. They may be called 'personnel managers', 'labour relations managers', 'staff officers', 'administration managers' or something more imaginative.

Self-check

Bearing in mind our definitions of 'industrial relations' and 'manager', what do you think a specialist 'industrial relations manager' might be responsible for?

ANSWER

The task of these specialist managers is hotly debated and varies from organisation to organisation. In general, however, they are concerned to monitor and control elements of the contract of employment and, as part of that, to handle the more important relationships with trade unions.

The debate about their job centres on whether or not they should take over parts of the line managers' task. Some managers argue that the IR specialists should help line managers with advice, but leave the decisions and even the action to the line manager. Others, often the specialists themselves, argue that if industrial relations are to be controlled, and as inconsistency is a major cause of problems in industrial relations, then the specialists must 'run the show'. They should make the decisions and, for example, run all meetings with the trade unions. Different organisations have taken different sides in this debate. They therefore have industrial relations specialists doing different jobs.

> *Activity*
>
> If you work in an organisation with a specialist department (personnel, industrial relations or whatever), ask to spend half an hour talking to the manager there. Ask him what he does; and listen to see which side of this debate his or her work falls – is he advisory to line managers, or does he take the decisions and handle trade union meetings himself? Check your decision with the specialist manager.

Levels of management

If different functions are important in management so are different levels. The 'hierarchy' of management, the way it is structured in different layers of authority, determines to a large extent each manager's task. I have worked in a small organisation where everyone was responsible to the managing director. In that company our functional tasks were the only determinant in our jobs. I have also worked, however, in organisations that employed many thousands, where some people reported to me and I reported to someone above me in the structure. Not only was I responsible to my boss for my work and my actions, I was also responsible for the work and results of the people who reported to me.

This is the typical pattern in modern organisations. Usually as soon as an organisation has become a handful of people in size there are different levels built in. This is so common that most of us question it rarely if at all. (You may indeed be wondering why we are spending time on the issue!)

It is when someone becomes responsible for someone else's work and activities that we can start speaking of them as a manager. And it is also when we start getting into the area of industrial relations.

Look at figure 2 which shows a typical hierarchical structure in an office.

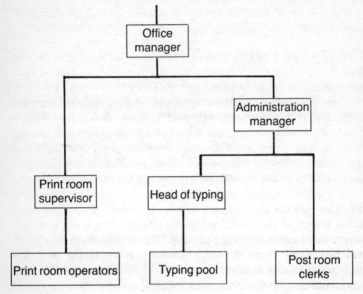

Figure 2.

Self-check

1 Is the head of typing in figure 2 responsible to the office manager for the quality and amount of typing that gets done?
2 Is the print room supervisor in figure 2 higher or lower in the hierarchy than the head of typing?

ANSWER

1 The chart shows that the head of typing reports directly to the administration manager, and only reports to the office manager *through* the administration manager. Eventual responsibility for everything in the office lies with the office manager, but in each individual item it is delegated through an intermediate layer of management.

2 We cannot tell from the chart about the respective positions of head of typing and print room supervisor. On the one hand the head of typing looks to be at the same level – and indeed the title sounds more impressive. But, on the other, the print room supervisor reports direct to the senior manager in the office.

Clearly we will need to look in detail at what managers do and how they compare themselves before we can judge a hierarchy in any particular case. Titles tell us very little.

These hierarchical differences have important implications for industrial relations. Look again at figure 2. It is likely that in practice the head of typing and the print room supervisor share a room with the employees they supervise and that they do some of the typing and print themselves. This means that they are in a very good position to understand the work and the people who do it. They will know how much an individual can be expected to do, how quickly they can do it, who is best at what. They will know which of their staff would be prepared to work late and which need extra overtime money. The higher-level managers will not know these details. They will have access to other information: how much they can afford to pay out in overtime payments and staff within their budget, or how the amount of typing or printing required may change over the next few months.

As with the functional differences, these hierarchical distinctions can give rise to tensions between the levels. Managers at senior levels may want to reduce staff costs for example, whereas the managers at the lower levels may find that their close relationships with employees and their knowledge of their personal need for extra cash makes it embarrassing for them to refuse overtime.

In general, managers at the lower levels are more aware of and concerned with the immediate work operation and the needs of individual members of staff. Managers at the higher levels are focused on the overall business requirements; they consider employees, where appropriate, as groups rather than individuals.

Activity

How will differences between departments or between levels of management be resolved? Think of some organisations you know about (the government might be a good case if you cannot think of any others).

ANSWER

What usually happens when a dispute between two departments cannot be resolved is that the matter is referred to a higher authority – to a more senior manager. Disputes between levels of manager are resolved when the higher-graded manager makes his decision. In practice differences of opinion between managers at the same level can get quite heated and are often referred up. Differences of opinion between managers at different levels may occur just as often, but are rarely seen. This is because most people realise that at the end of the day the senior manager's opinion will predominate; and in that case there is little point in pushing differences of opinion to a dispute.

The fact that authority in most employing organisations comes down from above means that we can see these organisation as pyramids:

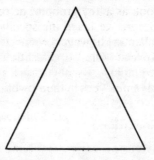

Our example of the office hierarchy could well form one small part of the picture. If you look back to p. 44 you will not need too much imagination to impose a pyramidal structure on that hierarchy. Nor would you require a lot of imagination to be able to fit that diagram into one corner of the triangle above, which represents the whole organisation. Authority in this diagram is located mainly at the apex – a managing director or chief executive perhaps. There is less authority at each successive level down the structure.

Departments, levels and industrial relations

What do all these departmental and functional differences mean for industrial relations? They are, in reality, crucial. Employees judge organisations largely on the basis of the way they are treated by their managers. This treatment will differ between individual managers, and it will often vary between departments. The hierarchical structure, however, means that in most organisations a management 'style' is established: managers who don't act in the way that is required are directed *by senior management* to change their behaviour. In this way the organisation develops a consistency of action amongst individual managers.

Employees react to the individual behaviour of their own manager. They also react to the overall management style of the organisation. Employee representatives and trade unions will be involved at both levels, as we shall see. But they too will be reacting to the behaviour of management.

Our discussion of management in industrial relations is by no means finished. The managers, and management, will recur throughout the book as a key group of actors on the industrial relations stage. Before we leave the specific focus upon them provided by this chapter, however, we need to examine briefly two related aspects: the organisations that represent managements, the employers' associations; and the unique position of managers as employees in their own right.

Employers' associations

Just as the employees in many organisations join together to form trade unions, so employers in many cases join together to form employers' associations. We will see that the number of trade unions has declined over the years with amalgamations. Employers' associations have also declined in numbers. Whereas the unions now have far more members than they did fifty or twenty-five years ago, however, the power and influence of the employers' associations is declining. There are now some 400 employers' associations in the UK active in industrial relations. They are as varied in their composition as the trade unions.

Activity

Write down the names of three major trade unions and three major employers' associations. If you have time, write down an explanation of what trade unions do (you should find that easy if you read the next chapter carefully), and what employers' associations do.

ANSWER

You will probably have found that it was quite easy to write down the names of three trade unions, and you know what they do. Unless you are something of an expert, you will have probably found it quite difficult to think of three employers' associations (the better-known ones include the Engineering Employers' Federation (EEF), the National Federation of Building Trades Employers (NFBTE), the Electrical Contractors' Association (ECA), the Chemical Industries Association (CIA), the Newspaper Publishers' Association (NPA) and the Local Authorities Conditions of Service Advisory Board (LACSAB)). It is also difficult to get any clear idea of what they do. These are somewhat secretive bodies; or, at least, they do not seek publicity.

What do we know about them? As with the trade unions, you should be wary of generalisation. They are all different – but there are some features common to most of them:

- membership and finance;
- organisational structure;
- staffing;
- activities.

Membership and finance are usually straightforward. Most associations are open to all employers in a particular industry (limited by geographical region in some cases), and aim to cover as many of them as possible. They sometimes restrict their membership to 'reputable businesses' and always insist that members agree to abide by the policy of the association. In practice this is not a very onerous requirement and it is far from unknown for employers to bend the rules and still remain members. The other requirement is, naturally, that the members pay their subscriptions. Most employers' associations are funded largely direct from subscription income.

Organisational structures are very varied. There are two broad types of association structure. Some associations are single national bodies which aim to recruit all the organisations in their industry directly. They may be public or private sector associations and they may or may not have branches or regional structures. Other associations recruit regionally and have an overall body at national level to which the associations belong: this format is typified by the Engineering Employers' Federation and its constituent local associations. It is mainly found in the private manufacturing sector.

Staffing of the associations varies considerably too. Some employ a large number of full-time staff specialising in all sorts of subjects; many employ just a small administrative secretariat; and a lot have no full-time staff and rely on local solicitors or accountants as central figures.

Activities of employers' associations are closely related to their staffing. What do they do? Much of their work falls outside industrial relations: legal and commercial advice, for example. Many of the associations are active in industrial relations, though, either in conducting negotiations with trade unions themselves or by providing specialist advice, or both.

Several of the employers' associations, usually the larger ones with full-time staff, negotiate directly with the trade unions, or with an equivalent federation of trade unions, to establish terms and conditions of employment for the whole industry. These will sometimes determine all the major aspects of the remuneration package and important conditions of work: they do in electrical contracting, for example. Sometimes they will determine most of the key aspects, and leave others to be negotiated locally. Usually, however, they set standards for basic pay and hours of work, and member firms are free to negotiate additional sums as and when they see fit.

Specialist advice is more ad hoc, given in response to requests from individual companies in most cases. Sometimes the association will issue guidance on how to cope with a new piece of legislation or a problem that is affecting several member organisations simultaneously. Very often the specialists will act as back-ups to, or even in place of, a firm's personnel department – advising on disciplinary and work-related issues, payment systems or responses to trade union demands. Often too the employers' association will be involved, with officials from the unions, in adjudicating on disputes that cannot be handled within the member organisation.

Self-check

The employers' associations have declined in membership and importance fairly steadily since the Second World War. Why do you think this might have occurred?

ANSWER

The main reason relates to the decline of national industrial bargaining and its reduced importance compared to bargaining at company level. This is partly because companies have begun to see the benefits of ensuring that the agreements they make with their staff fit the company's position, not that of the lowest common denominator for the industry as a whole. At the same time companies have begun to develop much more professional industrial relations departments of their own. There is a feeling amongst these departments that the employers' associations often take as their reference the interests of the greater number of less professional small companies.

The employers' associations are still an important part of the British industrial relations scene; but they are less important than they were.

The Confederation of British Industry

The employers also have their own national organisation representing them all. The trade unions' TUC is matched by the employers' CBI – the Confederation of British Industry.

The CBI represents over 10,000 members directly and speaks for all employing organisations. It has in membership individual companies in manufacturing and in commerce, covers the nationalised industries and includes employers' associations and commercial associations.

The CBI provides valuable services to, particularly, its smaller member organisations, but it has no real power over any of its members. Its main function is, as a conglomerate and uneasy coalition, to represent employing organisations to the rest of the nation in general and to government in particular.

Managers as employees

Most managers are also employees, paid a salary by their organisation and needing that salary to maintain their accustomed lifestyle. They are in most cases managers of some employees and themselves managed by someone else. Managers are therefore nearly always involved in industrial relations in at least two ways. They have a major impact on the working conditions of their own employees, and at the same time their own working conditions are influenced by their own boss.

A much lower proportion of managers than non-managerial employees is in membership of trade unions. Yet there are many thousands of managers, some of them highly paid, who are trade union members. There are indeed both separate unions for managers and separate sections of 'ordinary' unions which managers can join. Managers join trade unions, like any other employees, to obtain their support in discussions with *their* bosses about industrial relations issues.

In practice this rarely gives rise to any problems. This is a surprise to many Americans, for example, who believe that you are either part of the union or part of management. In Britain many people are happy to be both.

There are occasional conflicts of interest, but these are usually resolved amicably. In some companies, union members who are managers do not attend union meetings when the members are discussing the wage claim they will put to the company; but they attend all the others. They find it possible to act as good union members and yet not breach any confidences they obtain during work.

The real problems arise during an industrial dispute when individuals' loyalty as union members and as members of the management team may be in direct opposition. These can be very tense situations for the individual. Fortunately they are rare.

> ### Activity
>
> Look in the newspapers for details of a current dispute. Can you think of ways in which managers (or some managers) might gain if the trade unions achieve their demands? And how might the managers (or some of them) lose out if the unions are successful?

Management: in summary

We have seen then that management plays a central part in industrial relations, but that all managers are not the same. Differences in department and in level are important. The way these differences are resolved by senior management creates the 'management style' of the organisation as it appears to employees. And this decides whether industrial relations in the organisation are good or bad.

Some managements use employers' associations to negotiate and advise on key elements of their employees' terms and conditions of employment. We also noted that managers are also employees, and often union members. Overall, however, the management and the way they treat their subordinates are the vital factors in industrial relations.

3 | The trade unions

You have seen the headlines:

UNION TELLS CHANCELLOR, SPEND MORE

WILL THE UNIONS SAVE LABOUR?

CAR UNIONS IN ALL OUT STRIKE

UNION VOTES FOR CND

UNION SUPPORTS TORY COUNCILLOR

and a thousand more like them. What precisely are these unions? Are they all the same? What do they aim to achieve? How do they operate? How powerful are they? This chapter aims to help you answer these questions.

The first thing we need to be clear about is what we mean by a trade union.

Activity
What is a trade union? Attempt a definition.

ANSWER

There are all sorts of definitions of trade unions. These range from the very legalistic to the more practical. The legal definition of a trade union, in the Trade Union and Labour Relations Act 1974, states that a trade union is an organisation which 'consists wholly or mainly of workers of one or more descriptions and is an organisation whose principal purposes include the regulation of relations between workers of that description or those descriptions and employers or employers' associations'.

As in many other areas the law is here attempting to draw a clear line where there are many practical variations. It is saying that organisations either are or are not trade unions, whereas in practice organisations may be 'more or less' trade unions.

In practice, and probably in your definition too, there are a number of elements which constitute 'trade union-ness'. These are:

- That there is an organisation – not just a group of individuals.
- That the organisation exists to represent its members to employers (primarily) and to others such as the state, the press and the public.
- That the organisation's primary interest is in the terms and conditions of employment of its members, which it negotiates or wishes to negotiate with its members' employers.
- That the organisation is not controlled by those employers.
- That the organisation is prepared to arrange and coordinate the breaking of contracts of employment by its members (in strikes or other industrial action) where necessary.
- That the organisation is a member of the Trades Union Congress.
- That the organisation supports the Labour Party.

Many of the organisations that we read about in the newspapers will have all seven elements. Some will have less. Some organisations that we do not normally think of as trade unions will have many of these elements.

So the definition of a trade union is complex. It includes at the very least the idea of *bargaining collectively on behalf of its members with their employers*. Beyond that organisations may be more or less totally trade unions – and that has very little to do with their title, which may often use other words such as 'association', rather than 'union'.

In this book we are principally concerned with trade unions that have the first five elements. Most of these are also members of the TUC (the sixth element) and about half of them are affiliated to the Labour Party (the seventh). We shall deal with them starting with the members and working our way up to the national structures.

The trade union member

Picture for yourself (or draw if you are good at that) a trade union member. Get a clear impression of a single individual before you read on.

Are you looking at a middle-aged male manual worker in overalls, with perhaps a spanner in his dirty hands and a cigarette in the corner of his mouth, employed in some privately owned engineering works? He is the most common stereotype. He is not a typical trade union member.

Of course there are many trade union members just like that (and I can't give you any information about the number of trade unionists who smoke!). By the end of the 1970s, however, nearly a third of all trade union members were women: nearly 40 per cent of all trade union members were white-collar workers; the bulk of trade union members worked in the public sector. Furthermore these groups – women, white-collar workers and public sector employees – were becoming an ever-increasing proportion of the union membership. So if your picture of a trade unionist was one of a female clerical worker in the civil service, that too was an accurate view.

How many trade union members are there in Britain? It depends on our first, definitional point: which organisations you have included. It also depends on when you ask the question. The figure changes continually as new members join and some who are in the unions cease to be members. Let us use the official statistics presented by the government's Department of Employment and its predecessors.

Activity

Look at table 3. Write down two statements about the development of trade union membership that you can draw from that table.

Table 3. UK trade union membership at the end of each decade

1980	13 million
1970	11 million
1960	10 million
1950	9 million
1940	6½ million
1930	5 million
1920	8½ million
1910	2½ million
1900	2 million

ANSWER

Even from a simple table like this we can make important deductions:

- Trade union membership has tended to increase.
- It is higher now than ever.
- But it does not increase inevitably; sometimes it falls.
- The decades of the two world wars saw major increases.
- The inter-war depression saw a decrease.

The membership totals reached an all-time high of 13½ million in 1979, and the decline since 1979 is related to the increase in unemployment. This directs us to another measure: *trade union density*, or the percentage of the working population which is unionised. The total numbers may not mean too much unless we know the total number of the working population at the time. Again this has fluctuated throughout the century; by the end of the 1970s it stood at almost 60 per cent. In other words, six out of every ten members of the working population were members of a trade union.

Suppose we were to 'add in' some of the 'unions' which are not included in the Department of Employment statistics: doctors, lawyers, policemen and others which have at least elements of being organisations which negotiate collective terms and conditions. Suppose we take out of the ten members of the working population those who are self-employed, or in the armed forces. Then we can see that very few working people who could be in trade unions are not. Britain is a country in which most working people are trade union members; we are a highly unionised country.

Membership varies markedly between industries. In some traditional industries, such as mining, the docks and the railways, trade union membership is very high; in others, such as shopwork or agriculture, it is low. Fifty years ago there was no air transport industry and no computer industry – now union membership is very high in air transport, but very low in computers. Amongst teachers and nurses it has gone within living memory from low to high. So it changes over time as well as with industry. It also varies from company to company within the same industry and from group to group within the same company.

Why people join unions

Activity

Why do so many people join trade unions? If you are a union member try to remember why you joined and write a sentence that explains it. If not, try to imagine a situation in which you might join a trade union.

ANSWER

People will join trade unions for various reasons, some immediate and others more general. The immediate reasons might include the wish to influence a pay claim, a threat of redundancy, or some high-handed action by management. It is possible, of course, to respond to these situations by leaving employment. For most people, however, that is not a realistic option. They need a job and other jobs may not be easy to find. Furthermore most employees will have invested their time in the organisation they work for. Leaving will mean they lose seniority, their pensions may suffer, they will lose certain legal rights and so on. If leaving is not a realistic possibility, collective action through a trade union certainly is. There is much evidence that people join trade unions in increasing numbers when the economy is booming (to make sure they get their share) and in the initial stages of economic decline (for protection). But look at what happened between 1920 and 1930 in table 3: in the economic downturn of the Depression of the 1920s, membership declined even faster than jobs.

The more general reasons for joining a trade union will include the attitudes of colleagues at work, the influence of particular individuals, how 'acceptable' being a union member may be in a person's social group and how actively the unions are recruiting. Overall the extent of union membership is perhaps determined mostly by the attitude of government and the attitude of employers. If both are supportive, union membership will grow – as it did in the late 1970s. If both are antagonistic, it will decline – as it did in the early 1980s.

Joining a trade union is easy. There are far fewer hurdles to overcome than there are in joining a golf club, for example. It is not true, as some cynical commentators suggest, that a union will take anyone who is 'warm and willing' (i.e. alive and wants to join), but unions will generally want their membership to be as large as possible within the areas they cover – and some unions claim to cover all areas. In most circumstances, a potential member will find that there is a union which is recognised by fellow workers, management and other unions as being appropriate to that particular job.

If the rules governing which union you join and restrictions on who can join are less severe that those of a golf club, we should also add that it's a lot cheaper! A few unions fix their subscriptions at a percentage of their members' salaries – the pilots' union, BALPA, does it and, pilots being as well paid as they are, that makes BALPA a wealthy union. Most unions, however, have subscriptions fixed at certain weekly or monthly sums, adjusted when the union's policy-makers agree to do so. These subscriptions are often no more than the price of a pint of beer. They are significantly lower in Britain than in the rest of Europe. This in turn means that the resources available to the unions are meagre: the services, particularly the professional services, that they can provide are limited; and the unions rely heavily on their lay officials, the unpaid representatives amongst the membership who act as shop stewards or branch officials as well as working at their paid job. We will discuss them in more detail shortly.

Multi-unionism Some managers and several industrial relations experts are concerned about the extent of multi-unionism in Britain. By that they mean some employing organisation have to negotiate with several trade unions; this is usual in manufacturing or local government, for example. It is unusual in this country for just one union to represent all of one organisation's employees. Some experts point to the comparative strike records we looked at in Chapter 1 – compare the unions in Japan, where each company has its own union, or West Germany, where each of sixteen industries has its own union – and argue that multi-unionism is a cause. But as we said in Chapter 1, there is no simple cause. There is less multi-unionism in the United States and their strike record is much worse than Britain's.

We will look at multi-unionism again from the management viewpoint. From the point of view of the potential member, however, it is hardly important. In most cases it is clear which union he should join.

So far, then, we have considered a definition of trade unions by examining the elements that contribute to 'trade union-ness', the number and type of trade union members and the reasons that lead people to join. Before we move from discussing union members to examining the organisations they have set up, it is worth asking one more question about the membership.

Activity

Think back on what you have read so far. How do you imagine trade union members would judge whether their union was meeting their needs? Try to write down at least one test they would apply.

ANSWER

Trade unions provide a wide variety of services: they give legal support where necessary; they support members who want to take further education or some professional qualifications; they advise on safety matters; many unions even offer discounts on shopping or holidays!

There is very little room for doubt, however, that the members judge the union on what it achieves in negotiations at the workplace. It is the union's ability to defend its members from arbitrary management decisions, and to advance and improve the terms and conditions on which they are employed, that causes most people to join.

Of course there are some who will join the union because they believe in the labour movement or because they want to influence decisions made by the TUC. These individuals, who often form the backbone of the union's formal organisation, are rare, however. Because most individuals judge their union on its achievements at the workplace, the few who are committed to these wider ideals have a disproportionate influence at higher levels. Union members have been characterised as apathetic – not caring what the union does or says in their name. The truth is that the members are very concerned in their own workplace. But beyond that most members are indifferent to statements made by the distant figures theoretically in charge of their union.

The employee representative

Most members, when they talk about their union, are in practice thinking of their own local lay representatives. These representatives are fellow workers, employed by the organisation they work for as are all the other union members, but chosen to represent particular groups of them to management.

It is difficult to generalise about the employee representatives, or shop stewards as they are often known. Their functions and type are as varied as the members they represent. Even their titles are different: shop stewards, staff representatives, staff side committee members, corresponding members.

The selection of union representatives and their work

Activity

Before you read any further, write down what you think an employee representative or shop steward does. If you have them at your place of work try to outline what they in fact do; if you are not employed in such a workplace at present, use information you have been able to glean from the newspapers and television.

ANSWER

Whatever you have written you could be right, because the jobs of employee representatives are so varied. There are a few major tasks, however, which should be carried out by nearly all representatives:

- Making sure everyone who could be in the union is approached to join it.
- Maintaining interest and enthusiasm by keeping people informed about the work of the union.
- Alerting members to management actions and plans.
- Representing members' grievances and aspirations to management.

The representatives or shop stewards will carry out these tasks differently. One may just put notices on a noticeboard and speak to management only when a member has been disciplined; another may call regular meetings of the membership, meet frequently with management and negotiate wages and salaries. There is also a range of other tasks the representatives may perform: liaison with union officers, distribution of literature, attendance at safety or pension committee meetings and many more; but few representatives will do the full range. That would be a full-time job.

There are estimated to be about 300,000 union representatives in Britain. Most of them spend on average an hour or so a day of working time, for which they are paid as an employee, and perhaps as much again of their own time, for which they are not paid. Some of them, a few thousand, are in fact full-time. It is not uncommon in a factory or office to have a senior representative who is still paid 'wages' but who in fact works only as a representative. (These senior representatives are often called 'convenors'.)

The union rules place few restrictions on a representative, so the job is often what the individual makes of it.

Activity

Read the formal 'Functions of Shop Stewards' (issued by a union) and the 'Shop Steward's Credentials' (issued by a company) on pp. 62–3. These would be typical for a shop steward in manufacturing. What are the formal restrictions on individuals acting as a shop steward? List four.

Transport and General Workers' Union
Functions of shop stewards – rules and policies

For the purpose of representing membership on matters affecting their employment, a shop steward or equivalent representative shall be elected by the membership in a defined working area or at a branch meeting by a show of hands or ballot as may from time to time be determined.

Special elections shall be held on the requisition of the membership concerned or at defined periods, but in any case elections shall take place at least once every two years. The representative so elected shall be in compliance and act in accordance with union rules and policies.

The regional committee or its authorised subcommittee may have authority to withdraw credentials of a shop steward or equivalent representative in circumstances where it is considered that the representative is not acting in accordance with union rules and policies, subject to the right of appeal as provided for in these rules.

Shop stewards shall receive the fullest support and protection from the union, and immediate inquiry shall be undertaken by the appropriate trade group or district committee into every case of dismissal of a shop steward with a view to preventing victimisation, either open or concealed.

Shop stewards are not authorised to initiate or continue industrial action on behalf of the union. This authority is vested only in the general executive committee, its finance and general purposes committee and the general secretary.

Extract from TGWU shop steward's credential card, with acknowledgements.

Example of a shop steward's credentials

The company and trade union jointly agree on the following credentials for Mr/Ms . . . . who has been elected to represent the union members in the . . . . representational area on . . . . (date).

1 When acting in his/her union capacity he/she shall be subject to the rules and regulations of the union.
2 He/she accepts the duties laid down with the domestic and national procedure agreements in respect of the employees in the above representational area.
3 He/she agrees to abide, and to use his/her best endeavours to see that the members abide, by all agreements (of which he/she will receive copies) between the company and the union, whether

present or future, in particular the negotiating procedure for settling issues, hearing objection against disciplinary actions and dismissals.

4 He/she is assured that his/her average earnings will be maintained for the time he/she spends in carrying out his/her duties as defined by the agreements and his/her credentials.

5 Action taken by him/her in good faith in pursuance of his/her duties shall in no way affect his/her employment with the company.

6 In all other respects he/she shall conform to the same working conditions as other employees.

ANSWER

You may have noted:

- They should comply with union rules and policies.
- They may not initiate or continue industrial action on behalf of the union.
- They must abide by relevant agreements and try to ensure that their members do so too.
- They will, when not acting as a shop steward, conform to the same rules as their workmates.

These are hardly onerous restrictions, particularly when we remember that even these are not observed. Most strikes, for example, are inpromptu events, over before the formal union structure gets to hear about them. Employee representatives rarely receive much more than this in the way of formal advice on how to do their jobs. Only a minority of them receive training for the task, although many are given a handbook. Most of them develop their activities through a combination of learning-by-watching (either the shop stewards they replaced or a senior shop steward or convenor) and from their own assessment of what needs to be done. Little wonder that the job differs so noticeably from one representative to another.

Selection The extract from the TGWU shop steward's credential card (p. 62) also refers to how the representatives are chosen. In theory this is by means of frequent elections. In practice these are the exception. There is not a great deal of competition for a difficult and often thankless job which involves a lot of time.

Furthermore it is a job which puts the individual in the position of trying to satisfy the conflicting expectations of the managers they work for and the colleagues they work with. In most cases only one person stands for election, and they have often had to be pushed into the job.

Again it is difficult to generalise. The election or selection of representatives varies as does the way they work for their members, the extent of their job, and a number of other factors that we have not the space to discuss in detail – such as the number of members they represent (which may range from a handful to hundreds), their relationship with their full-time union officials or their importance in their organisation.

Work of a representative To return to the earlier question, it is difficult to say precisely what each employee representative does. As well as serving his or her workmates, the shop steward is also a representative of the union and an employee. These obligations will pull in different directions and it is often the unpredictable results of the tradition of the workplace and the character of the individual which will determine their approach.

The workplace representatives are chosen by their colleagues to discuss, argue and negotiate on their behalf with their own management. The representative also meets with representatives from other workgroups. They may be from a different part of the same office or factory or they may be from other workplaces of the same employer in different parts of the country. The majority of representatives are members of local committees: staff side committees, office representative committees, joint shop stewards' committees. These will often include representatives from other unions as well as other work areas. Some will be members of wider arrangements: 'combine committees', which include representatives of all the unions and all the workplaces covered by one employer. In many unions the workplace representatives attend regular 'industrial conferences' of their union to consider the union's policy in relation to the particular industries they come from.

The representatives, or most of them, will also be involved in frequent discussions with management. Some of these discussions will take place with senior members of the management team, directors or board members.

These meetings, with other workgroups' representatives, with other people in the union hierarchy and with managers, mean that the representative has more information than his fellow workers and often a somewhat different perspective. The representative can then cease to be a mere mouthpiece for the workgroup and can develop a position as leader, influencer and persuader.

This is where the representative's position becomes controversial. Some newspapers at least seem to believe that employee representatives are leading their colleagues astray. They seem to believe this in particular when the representatives are called shop stewards!

Review

What is your view? Take five minutes to think about this section on employee representatives (reread it if you want to). Think about any that you have known. Are they in general a positive or a negative factor in industrial relations?

As a final word here about the employee representative consider this quote from the Royal Commission on Industrial Relations which reported in 1968. Its conclusions are backed up by more recent research:

Shop stewards are rarely agitators pushing workers towards unconstitutional action. In some instances, they may be the mere mouthpiece of their workgroups. But, quite commonly, they are supporters of order exercising a restraining influence on their members.

The Commission's Report adds:

For the most part the shop steward is viewed by others, and views himself, as an accepted and even moderating influence; more of a lubricant than an irritant.*

*Report of the Royal Commission on Trade Unions and Employers' Associations (chairman: Lord Donovan), 1968.

Union structure

So far we have said little about the formal union structures. This is because for the members the union is usually seen. as the representative, and most representatives are integrated only very loosely into the formal structure of the union. Many union rulebooks still give only very scant mention to these crucial components of the union's structure.

Those representatives that do get more involved in the union outside the workplace often do so in other positions, as branch secretaries or committee members. It is to these more formal structures that we turn now.

The branches

Self-check

To what extent can we usefully generalise about trade union members and shop stewards? A lot, somewhat or hardly at all?

ANSWER

By now it should be clear that we can hardly generalise at all without risking some large inaccuracies. As the members and representatives form the bedrock of the union it follows that we will not be able to generalise about the official union structures any more easily.

There are a number of broad similarities, particularly amongst the unions that have at least the first six of our elements of trade-union-ness. In the first place they operate through some form of branch structure. Branches are the immediate unit to which all members belong. Most are based on a geographical area or workplace, some are occupational (for instance, senior staff branch), others are based on an industry. They all have regular, often monthly, meetings which all members are entitled to attend – but which few actually do.

Activity

Why are attendances at branches usually so low?
Write out a sentence giving your reasons.

ANSWER

The low level of attendance is hardly suprising, if our understanding of the members' objectives is correct. They are mainly interested in the union as a negotiating body at the workplace, not in it as a formal bureaucracy. They put their views through the shop steward or representative, not through the branch.

It is through the branches that the shop stewards or employee representatives are linked to the formal union structure. Many of the representatives also hold some branch office: branch chairman, branch secretary, treasurer. In the public sector, which tends to have workplace-based branches, 'employee representative' and 'branch official' are often just different titles for the same job.

What does the branch do? It is often used, particularly in the older unions which recruit mainly manual workers, as a financial unit, where the shop stewards can pay in the subscriptions collected at their place of work. Generally speaking, however, 'subs' are increasingly being deducted from the employees' pay by the company, which then passes the total sum on to the union offices. This is the 'check-off' system.

One of the key functions of the branch is exchange of information. In workplace-based branches this will be information about the activities of a particular employer, or perhaps about different groups of managers in a large public sector undertaking. In geographically based branches this will be comparative information so that the members can assess how their terms and conditions look alongside those in other companies.

The branch can play an important role in coordinating the activities of the members. It is often the branch that plans approaches to management on a variety of topics, gathers material for wage and salary claims and organises action in the event of a dispute.

The branch is also the fundamental building block in the structure of the trade union. At the branch members will discuss and debate any issue that they themselves decide to be important; here also the resolutions which eventually form the policy of the whole union will be formulated. Each union will have its own arrangements about how these issues are progressed up from the branch level but all unions are committed to the concept that they are democratic organisations, controlled and directed by the membership. The control and direction are based on the branches.

Regional structure

The actions of the branches are progressed through or reviewed by the next level of the union hierarchy. For most of at least the larger unions the regional (or divisional or district) level is an important intermediary between the branches and the head-quarters. It is at this level that most unions place their junior level full-time officials. In a number of the unions, particularly those that have the official elected by the members rather than appointed by headquarters, these regional posts can command a good deal of power and often a substantial independence of the directions of the headquarters officials.

Other unions, some of those in the civil service, for example, do not have a regional structure at all. In these cases the branches are grouped into sections covering similar types of branch throughout the country. Other unions again, such as the Transport and General Workers, have both regional and sectional groupings.

Activity

If you are in a union, draw out you own union's organisational structure in diagrammatic form. If you are not a union member choose a union that interests you and do the same thing. You will be able to draw your information from the union's own rule book and other publications or from the public library which will provide you with union directories. Try writing direct to the union's headquarters for information.

Trade union headquarters

The headquarters of the union will in most cases house a general secretary, responsible for the administration of the union, some national officers and a number of service departments. These might include some or all of the following: membership and organisation department, research department, a computer section, a finance department, training and education departments, public relations, information and publications departments, health and safety sections, insurance and superannuation departments and a secretariat.

Depending on the size and complexity of the union, and upon its history and constitutional arrangements, headquarters can loom very large in union affairs.

General secretary Whereas for most members their union is the shop steward, for most of the media the union is the general secretary. These are the names and faces that we see in our newspapers each morning and on our television screens each night. Their real power will vary. In a union like the National Union of Seamen whose members are spread around the globe, often away from the UK for long periods of time, there is little alternative to a powerful general secretary running the union and negotiating most of the major deals. Another union which has superficial similarities, the British Airline Pilots' Association, in fact has many highly educated, articulate and literate members with plenty of time available to get involved in many of the union's activities. Here the general secretary has less opportunity to 'run the show' his way.

General secretaries are often elected by the full membership of the union. In most unions, once elected, they are in post for life. Some unions require their general secretaries to stand in regular elections every few years. And in others the general secretary is appointed, not elected.

Other officials Below the general secretary there will be other officials. A few unions, like the Amalgamated Union of Engineering Workers (AUEW) and the Electrical Electronic Telecommunications and Plumbing Union (EETPU), have full-time executive councils elected directly by the membership. Most unions have a number of national officials working from headquarters

Full-time officials are not, in most cases, elected. But in some unions, particularly the more traditional craft unions, all the full-time officials are elected subject to periodic re-election. In other unions only the very top posts, such as general secretary, are elected – and that election often lasts for life. In some unions all the officials are appointed without election; in others some are elected and some appointed.

Elections usually take place at branch meetings. As we have already noted, these are often attended only by a small number of active members. Although others could attend, the system has nonetheless been criticised as being undemocratic. Some unions have moved to postal ballots sent to and from the members' homes. The government has made money available to the unions who wish to use this more expensive approach.

Activity

Why should a union wish to appoint its full-time officials and why should it elect them? Think of two advantages for each approach.

ANSWER

The debate focuses on accountability versus efficiency. The promoters of appointment argue that this enables unions to:

- select high-quality officials even if they have no background in the union;
- select younger, more vigorous, better educated officials;
- give officials job security and a career path;
- select women, blacks and others who can make a contribution to the union but might not win a ballot;
- have officials who will where necessary lead the union members to accept unpopular decisions.

Those who argue in favour of electing and re-electing officials point to the effects of:

- ensuring that the officials remain accountable to the members, who can 'de-elect' them if they do not meet their wishes;
- requiring the officials to keep in touch with and reflect their constituents' concerns and ambitions;
- ensuring that every aspirant for union office has done his or her share of the more mundane union jobs;

- getting officials who are committed to the union's cause and not to their own careers.

This is a continuing debate.

Activity

If you know any active trade unionists ask them whether they support election or selection of union officials; then try to put the arguments of the other side.

Whether appointed or elected, the job of the full-time officials is to carry out the union's policy. They do not make that policy. In all unions the supreme policy-making body consists of a group of elected lay members. Sometimes they will meet as national conferences; once a year or once every two years. These may be gatherings of some hundreds of members representing everyone in the union. Sometimes they will be national committees; smaller groups but again of lay members. Most unions have a system whereby resolutions can be originated in the branches and passed up through the regional or sectional structures to industrial interest-group conferences or to the full policy-making conference. The extent to which these policy-making bodies do in practice restrict the action of full-time officials varies. There are certainly instances of officials deciding to resign after finding themselves continually at odds with key policies.

In all there are over 400 unions in Great Britain. They employ over 3,000 full-time officials. Most of these officials are drawn from the membership they represent, although, especially amongst the white-collar unions and in the civil service, there are an increasing number of well-educated 'professional' officials being appointed. These officials, with one or two exceptions, are not highly paid. They do important and demanding jobs that keep them involved well into the evenings, attending branch or committee meetings or recruiting and negotiating. They often work weekends, on union training courses or at conferences, and most of them do a lot of travelling around the country. There can be little doubt that the vast majority of them are dedicated people working hard to support and improve the lot of their members.

There are over twelve million members. Other countries, like West Germany and the United States, have fewer members but more full-time officials.

> *Review*
>
> Look back at the chapter so far. How can so few full-time officials hope to provide a service to so many members?

The answer is that they can't. The unions rely heavily on the 300,000 lay officials (branch officers and workplace representatives), and now over half as many workplace safety representatives too. These people are the backbone of the trade union movement.

The spice of life

If it is true that variety is the spice of life then anyone studying the trade unions will hardly lack tasty titbits of information. There is almost no blanket statement that can be made about trade unions that will not need to be qualified in the case of some of them.

> *Activity*
>
> Keep your newspapers for three or four days. Go through them and ring all mentions of trade unions that you can find. Then for each mention ask yourself:
>
> ● Which union(s) are they talking about?
> ● Whom within the union(s) are they referring to: members, lay representatives, local officials, headquarters officials, the general secretary?

These questions are useful ones to ask every time you hear anyone generalising about 'the unions'.

'Feds' and 'confeds'

Unions often act independently, but they can also operate jointly. There are arrangements within many organisations for unions to work together, going under a variety of names, such as joint shop stewards committees or the trade union side of a particular local council. There are joint groupings at national or industrial level in which, for example, all the Post Office unions or all the shipbuilding and engineering unions meet and liaise on a regular basis. Such bodies are known as 'federations' or 'confederations'.

The Trades Union Congress

There are over 400 trade unions in the UK registered with the certification officer. At the end of the 1970s those unions had well over twelve million members. Just over 100 of those unions are affiliated to the main national grouping of unions: the Trades Union Congress, or TUC as it is more commonly known. These unions include well over 90 per cent of all members.

We are so used to the TUC appearing in our newspapers and on television that we are often unaware of how unusual it is. There are only a minority of countries that have a single organisation to represent and speak so authoritatively for all their trade unions. Other countries have national federations that represent much smaller percentages of the work-force, or are split along religious, political or occupational lines. The British TUC covers all the major and most medium-sized unions in the country and also includes a good representation of the small ones. It is a single body speaking for most trade unionists.

The Trades Union Congress does play some part in the occasional membership disputes between unions. In these rare, but often bitter, disputes as to who should recruit certain members the TUC now has a well-established procedure for settlement. The TUC also provides a great deal of information to its constituent unions. And it provides an extensive shop steward and safety representative training programme through a range of further education facilities.

These are valuable but peripheral services. The main function of the TUC lies not in its concern with the affairs of its own constituents but in its position as spokesman and representative for the union movement: in its outward rather than its inward task. The TUC has little real power over its member unions but it has a great deal of influence as the voice of the labour movement.

Very few major governmental decisions are taken without some consultation with the Trades Union Congress, though governments differ in how much they allow the TUC view to influence them. The TUC is represented on many important committees and public bodies. It has a major input into the financing, organisation and policies of the Labour Party (see Chapter 4).

It is a mistake to see the TUC as an overall umbrella organisation controlling its members. Rather it is a mouthpiece for the policies and influence that its members wish to pursue.

TUC structure

What is the structure that the TUC has developed to ensure that it represents its member unions' views accurately? Not surprisingly the TUC's internal arrangements mirror many of the aspects we have seen amongst the unions. Instead of individual members, the TUC has unions: paying and sending delegates to the annual congress on the basis of size.

The congress meets alternately in Blackpool or Brighton, in September of each year, to establish policy. The votes of each union are weighted according to its size. This is known as the 'block vote': each union voting as if all its members were in agreement on the issue under debate. Organisationally the TUC is led by the general council – the fifty-two senior union officials who meet monthly at the TUC headquarters in London to conduct business between the annual congresses. This is in practice mostly undertaken by a number of sub committees and the specialist staff that service them. The specialist full-time staff are, as are most unions, headed by a general secretary. The TUC does have a regional structure but it is very weak. It also has some 400 'trades councils' operating as its local agents. Their success depends on the enthusiasm of the local union officials, lay and full-time, and some are extremely active. The links to the national body are, however, often weak.

Self-check

To what extent are the functions and powers of the Trades Union Congress similar to those of the CBI outlined in Chapter 2?

ANSWER

In many respects they are identical. Comparing our discussion of the TUC with that of the CBI in Chapter 2 we find that in both cases:

- The main function is to represent the views of member organisations.
- The main target for influence is government.
- Special services are provided for members, particularly for smaller member organisations.
- Very little power is exercised over members, except by persuasion.

We should remember of course that there are also major differences of structure and policy reflecting the different organisations that each body covers.

4 | Industrial relations and the state

When we discussed definitions of industrial relations we found that one of the parties that would often be involved was the state (see p. 13). To understand the way the state is involved we need to appreciate:

- the state as a major employer;
- the state as economic manager;
- the state as law-maker;
- the state as the provider of specialist services.

We will consider each of these aspects in turn.

The state is the third party involved in industrial relations. Its involvement may not be so direct or so obvious as the involvement of the trade unions or of management but its position may be even more important. The state sets the framework within which industrial relations exists. It decides the form that industrial relations will take. This is clear to the unions and to employers and the managers who run their undertakings. We cannot understand industrial relations until we understand the part played by the state.

For some readers, those of you employed in industrial sectors in which the state is deeply involved, such as the civil service, local authorities, the national health service or the nationalised industries, this chapter will be central to understanding what is happening at your workplace. For others this chapter will form part of the background to understanding British industrial relations.

Self-check

Why should we use the somewhat unfamiliar word 'state' in this context, rather than, say, 'government'? Try to think of at least one reason.

ANSWER

There are two main reasons. The first is that 'state' is more neutral: it does not refer to any particular party or power group, whereas the word 'government' may well be read as meaning the group that is in office now. The second reason is that it is a wider term: it covers all the various organisations that are directly employed by us, by the taxpayers. Thus it includes the machinery and employees of the government in the civil service and related advisory and specialist organisations – there are quite a few of these in industrial relations.

Review

The concept of the 'state' normally also includes such employees of the country as the police and the armed forces. Refer back to our definitions (p. 13). Take a few minutes out to consider whether these aspects of the state are involved in 'industrial relations'.

The state as employer

Self-check

Consider Table 4. Approximately what percentage of the workforce is employed by the state (a) directly and (b) indirectly?

Table 4. Employment by sectors

	Percentage of employment
Agriculture, forestry and fishing	1.6
Mining and quarrying	1.5
Manufacturing	30.1
Construction	5.6
Gas, electricity and water	1.5
Transport and communications	6.6
Distribution	12.3
Insurance, banking, etc.	5.6
Professional and scientific services	16.4
Miscellaneous	10.1
National government	2.7
Local government	4.3
Armed forces	1.4

It depends to some extent how we define such words as 'employed;, 'directly' and 'indirectly'. We could argue that between 10 per cent and 20 per cent of all employees are employed directly by the state, depending upon whether we included local authority workers or not.

We could argue too that a further 10 per cent to 20 per cent are employed indirectly by the state, depending upon which nationalised and semi-nationalised companies we included, and whether we added in organisations such as the motorway construction companies which work almost entirely for the state.

In addition it would be possible to claim that there are a substantial number of firms in the private, non-state sector which provide goods or services, like uniforms, equipment or machinery, almost entirely to nationalised industries such as the National Coal Board, the health service, the fire service or the armed forces. Perhaps their employees should be counted in too. Whichever way you add up the figures, it is clear that the state is not only a major employer in Britain now; it is by a long way the dominant employer in the country.

The Whitley Committee

The civil service and many other parts of the state machinery conduct their industrial relations on the Whitley pattern. The Whitley Committee was set up and reported immediately after the First World War. The committee was asked to make recommendations about industrial relations, and its brief, 27-page report has probably had more impact on public sector industrial relations than the millions of words that have been written since. Whitley and his committee recommended a system of joint councils at national, district and local level, meeting frequently to discuss industrial relations issues. Employers and unions would each be represented on all levels, and neither would be allowed to outvote the other. Thus any changes to the employment situation would have to be agreed by both sides or they would not take place. These recommendations were adopted wholeheartedly by the government of the day. For more than half a century all aspects of employment have been discussed through just such joint machinery in nearly all areas where the state is directly involved.

Requirements to establish Whitley-style machinery were included by successive governments in Acts of Parliament setting up new services or nationalising certain industries. Sadly, although the Whitley Committee had aimed its recommendations rather more at the private than the public sector, its ideas were taken up in full in only a minority of cases. And in many they were simply ignored.

Self-check

What might be some of the advantages that led the Whitley Committee to recommend such a system of joint consultation? You should be able to think of two or three in a couple of minutes.

ANSWER

The advantages might include:

- The recognition of the legitimacy of trade union interest in a wide range of subjects, combined with a formal channel for that interest to be expressed.
- The potential flexibility of the system (realised in practice).
- Regular meetings at all levels to improve communication and reduce the possibility of conflict over important issues.
- Stable and continuing procedures to reduce the need or demand for non-constitutional ways of raising issues (strikes or go-slows, for example).

Despite these advantages the state has over recent years had its problems in industrial relations. The last decade has seen industrial disputes not only in the traditionally difficult nationalised industries, such as the mines, the steel industry and the railways, but in many other areas. Groups of workers who had previously been thought to be antagonistic to trade unions became involved in industrial action: civil servants, firemen, local authority workers, nurses.

Activity

Why should this increase in union activity among such groups of state employees have taken place? Can you think of any reasons that explain this change?

ANSWER

Of course, if you have discovered the answer to that particular question you have solved a problem that has been perplexing governments and commentators for a long time. It is a complex area and there are certainly a great variety of reasons for this increased tendency to use industrial action in the public sector. The reasons include:

- Increasing pressure by government on public sector costs (see p. 81 later in this chapter).
- Increasing numbers of younger workers employed in the public sector, bringing in different objectives, educational backgrounds and philosophies.
- Declining status of many of these sectors – employees in them are now seen as just another part of the workforce rather than as a sub-élite.
- The impact of growing prosperity in the private sector which had led to a relative decline in the financial position of many public sector workers.
- The impact of pay policies (see p. 83 later in this chapter) which have been most restrictive in those areas most under government control.

These partial explanations leave us a long way short of understanding why there is industrial action; that requires an examination of each instance as it occurs. They do help us to understand, however, why the public sector is becoming more like the private sector in its industrial relations. It sometimes looks much worse, of course. Because there is only one employer, because there are large numbers of employees involved and because action in the public sector usually has a very direct effect upon the public, strikes here attract a lot of press attention.

In many ways the state, as employer, has peculiar difficulties to face, as the last sentence indicates. The state is not able to act as other employers do. There is a political dimension. The low wages paid in many branches of the civil service, in the health service and by local authorities seem to be acceptable to the general public. It would not be seen as acceptable, however, for public sector employees to be 'sacked' arbitrarily. In employment terms alone, the state has led the field in such areas as trade union recognition, employment guarantees and pensions provisions.

And, of course, with so much employment directly or indirectly controlled by the state, its wages and salaries and indeed all aspects of its industrial relations are an important part of its economic management function.

The state as economic manager

One of the prime duties of the state is to manage the economy. This has an indirect effect on industrial relations, as well as some very direct implications.

We will look at these implications; at how the state has affected industrial relations in its attempts to manage the economy (particularly through incomes policies), and at the relationship between industrial relations and politics and the objectives that the state may be trying to achieve.

Self-check

Apart from the state's direct involvement in wage and salary negotiations, how might its general management of the economy influence industrial relations? Try to think of two or three ways.

ANSWER

Once we start considering the interrelationship of the national economy and industrial relations we realise that we are thinking about an extensive and complex area. Any comprehensive summary would be longer than this book. To give a few examples:

● Government action which affects employment will affect the bargaining power of the unions, or might make the parties concentrate on different issues, like redundancy agreements.
● Changes to national insurance might encourage or discourage individuals who want to become self-employed.

- Government support of subsidies for particular industries or companies will change employment prospects there, and in supplier organisations.
- Changing inflation rates will have a key influence on employees' expectations in the annual pay negotiations.

You may have thought of many others.

We should also remember that because the state owns or controls much of the British economy it has a very immediate influence over it.

Self-check

(Without turning back to p. 78.) What are the areas of employment controlled by the state? Check back once you've written an answer.

Of course the extent of the state's ownership is a matter of political debate. There is a fundamental difference in the Conservative Party's approach to this topic, which emphasises the need for market competition and decentralisation, from that of the Labour Party, which emphasises planning and coordination. Whichever party is in power, however, the UK is likely to be running a 'mixed economy' with a substantial proportion of the economy under direct government ownership and another substantial section privately owned.

I do not want to leave you with any impression that the government has little or no influence in those sectors which it does not own. Many businessmen believe that the government's influence is crucial; it determines the rates at which money can be borrowed, the opportunities to expand, the industries that will be viable in the future. The actions of the state do not, much to the chagrin of some, determine which companies will be successful and which will fail. They do, however, set the framework within which all companies operate.

All these factors will affect industrial relations within organisations, though they will affect them somewhat indirectly. The state's management of the economy does, however, also relate very directly to industrial relations. Even before the Second World War the state was liable to get involved in industrial relations as part of its attempts to manage the economy. Since 1945 such involvement has been seen as vital: most politicians would echo Conservative Prime Minister Edward Heath, who said: 'I consider industrial relations to be absolutely crucial to economic progress.'*

In particular most governments, and not just those in Britain, have seen the control of the financial outcome of collective bargaining as central to the economy. By the outcome I mean, of course, the wages and salaries that employers and employees negotiate. In practice this has meant that governments have attempted to influence the result of those negotiations.

Activity

What means might government employ to influence the result of negotiations? Try to think of at least two separate methods.

ANSWER

Governments have used a variety of methods. These include:

- exhortation and persuasion;
- statutory laws backed by legal sanctions on those who exceed the laid-down limits;
- negotiating themselves with the central employees' and employers' bodies (the TUC and the CBI) and leaving it to them, and to public opinion, to control the negotiators;
- using their control over the public sector to limit pay increases there, with the expectation that increases in the private sector will follow suit.

It is usual for a combination of these methods to be involved.

Incomes policies

These attempts to restrict the financial outcome of collective negotiations are given the generic title of 'incomes policies'. They are the subject of a fierce and continuing political and

*Preface to the Conservative Party pamphlet *Fair Deal at Work 1968*.

economic debate. Argument centres on a few key questions:

- Do incomes policies work? Or are wage and salary levels a response to economic conditions rather than a prime cause of them?
- Are incomes policies fair? Why should earned income be restricted when unearned income from shareholding, etc. is not? Isn't it easier for the highly-paid to protect their increases by taking them in kind (such as a bigger car rather than more cash) whereas the low-paid have no option?
- Are incomes policies effective? Do they in fact achieve their objectives?

Incomes policies are a subject of much debate and are seen differently by different negotiators. On both the trade union and the companies sides there are those who see incomes policies as the opposite of negotiation: 'If a 3 per cent limit is set, we just get together and rubber stamp the 3 per cent for a particular organisation.' Others see it as a challenge: 'If we're restricted to 3 per cent on the pay package, what else can we do?' This group would start looking at non-pay benefits such as cheap travel to work or at new areas of negotiation like increasing training opportunities.

It seems that precise incomes policies, enforced by law if necessary, work well only in certain circumstances. These are:

- Where the state exercises a great deal of control over many aspects of working life, as it does in the Communist countries of Eastern Europe or some of the capitalist countries of the Far East.
- Or where countries have small working populations and a high degree of 'social consensus' (such as Holland or Scandinavia) or agreement about society's objectives.

Incomes policies work less well in large, complex societies where there is a much lower degree of social consensus. Britain is just such a country.

Table 5. A history of incomes policy

1948–50
Wage freeze with exceptions for skill differentials, lower-paid workers and undermanned industries.

1956
A prices plateau policy. Exhortation to employers to restrain price increases which it was hoped would result in lower wage demands. 1957 establishment of the Council on Prices, Productivity and Incomes (Cohen Committee).

1961
Imposition of a 'pay pause' in the public sector.

1962
Introduction of a 'guiding light' of 2½ per cent for movements in money incomes. National Incomes Commission established.

1964–70
Productivity, prices and incomes policy. Laid down 'norms' for price and money income movements with certain exceptions (productivity bargaining, low pay, relativities and labour shortages). Policy administered by National Board for Prices and Incomes. After July 1966 statutory policy (Prices and Incomes Acts).

June 1970–Oct. 72
Informal incomes policy operating in the public sector (commonly referred to as the 'N–I' policy).

Nov. 1972–Mar. 74
Statutory prices and Incomes policy. Policy enforced by the Prices Commission and the Pay Board which worked to a prices and pay code respectively. Set pay limits on the basis of a flat-rate and/or percentage increase with a maximum absolute increase.

Sept. 1974–Aug. 75
The 'Social contract', mark 1, between trade unions and Labour government. Unions to restrict pay increases to the maintenance of real wages in a twelve-month period in return for tax changes, price controls and the restoration of free collective bargaining.

Aug. 1975–July 76
The 'social contract', mark 2. £6 per week maximum increase allowed.

Aug. 1976–July 77
The 'social contract', mark 3. Pay increases to be limited to 5% with a minimum increase of £2.50 per week and a maximum of £4 per week.

Aug. 1977–July 78
Earnings increase to be limited to 10%. Policy to be enforced via restricted price increases, cash limits, withdrawal of government contracts and selective financial assistance.

Aug. 1978–July 79

5 per cent guideline with minor exemptions (low pay to be brought up to £44.10 per week earnings, productivity deals which are self-financing, certain groups with anomalies – police, university teachers, etc.). Policy to be enforced via cash limits, government controls and selective financial assistance. Permitted price increase control dropped since government did not have parliamentary majority to obtain the necessary parliamentary approval to get the legislation extended.

July 1979 onward

Series of successively reduced limits on the public sector, enforced via strict monetary controls. Exhortation to the private sector to do likewise.

What is common to most countries in which incomes policies can be seen to be effective is that they have a centralised bargaining structure (i.e. pay and conditions are set for everyone by just a few overall meetings). Here we need only note that in Britain and other countries with decentralised bargaining (i.e. a large number of negotiations over pay and conditions) incomes policies have to grapple with many conflicting criteria.

Activity

What problems do you think the government might face in establishing an incomes policy? Try to think of two or three separate problems.

ANSWER

You may have noted:

- how to reconcile simplicity and the ability to control with flexibility (if everyone gets just 3 per cent that's easy to check; if all sorts of groups are allowed more or less, it becomes more difficult);
- how to reconcile strictness with fairness (if everyone is allowed 3 per cent this year, should workers who got no increase last year be allowed more?);
- how to reconcile help for the low paid with the need to maintain differentials (3 per cent of £5 is only £0.15; 3 per cent of £1,000 is £30 – so the worse off get relatively even poorer);

- how to reconcile timings with justice (if your factory and mine both agree to a 10 per cent increase, and yours came into effect last week and mine next, I will not be too happy with a 3 per cent limit imposed *this* week).

There are other problems. In particular, an increasing proportion of the income of many white-collar workers and managers is being taken in non-wage items – private medical insurance, motor cars, season-ticket allowances, luncheon vouchers, bonuses. These are difficult items for anyone wanting to monitor wage increases to control.

The political connection

Despite the above problems, many argue that some sort of incomes policy is either inevitable or desirable. It is a debate that has many political overtones, so this is a good time at which to raise a new issue:

- *What is the relationship between industrial relations and politics?*

Self-check

Can you remember the first point we made about industrial relations in Chapter 1? Could we make the same point about politics?

ANSWER

You'll remember that we emphasised, right at the beginning of our analysis of industrial relations, that the subject is value-laden. How you react to events, and the overall view that you will take of the subject, is strongly influenced by your values. The same is true for politics. A Conservative Party supporter will be able to put forward clear and coherent reasons why anyone (or indeed, everyone!) should also support the Conservative Party's views. And a Labour Party supporter, why everyone should support the Labour Party, and so on. In fact there can be very few people who took a conscious decision to weigh up all the evidence and 'choose' a party; most people find themselves generally in agreement with one party or another and then start to find reasons for their support.

What has this got to do with industrial relations? The same values which lead an individual to support one political party or another will often lead that individual to take a view of industrial relations that coincides with the views of the chosen party. There is seen to be an affinity of views between the Labour Party and the trade unions and between the Conservative Party and the employers. The other parties are not linked in this way.

We have already noted (p. 73) that Britain is unusual in Europe in having trade unions and political parties which, with the single exception of Northern Ireland, are not divided on religious lines. But, whether we like it or not, there are divides.

Many trade unions expressly avoid political affiliation – less than a half are linked to a political party. All those that are linked, however, are linked to the Labour Party.

Activity

Why should the trade unions and the Labour Party be allies? Try to think of at least three different reasons.

ANSWER

The links between the two are ideological, historical, financial and economic. Ideologically both are committed to increasing equality, to social ownership and to democratic controls. Historically, the Labour Party was founded by the trade unions to fight, amongst other things, for trade union rights. Financially, the trade unions provide the bulk of the Labour Party's income and a lot of organisational support. And in terms of management of the economy the trade unions and the Labour Party have similar objectives.

Activity

Take a couple of minutes to think about the links between the owners and managers of businesses and the Conservative Party. Do they have similar links?

ANSWER

Indeed they do. Both are ideologically committed to the present capitalist economy in which private businesses may thrive, and to the importance of incentives (in terms of financial reward) for those who invest their money. Historically, there are links between them going back several centuries. Financially, businessmen, big and small, are the major supporters of the Conservative Party. And again this party and owners and managers of business have similar objectives in the management of the economy.

The position of the other parties, such as the Liberal Party and the Social Democratic Party, is less clear or perhaps, they might say, more independent. Nevertheless their view of the way the state should manage the economy will be crucial to the way they are viewed by businessmen and trade unions.

Let us move down from our abstraction, the 'state', to the various party governments that have been in power. Each will, amongst other things, be attempting to meet general economic objectives.

Activity

What general economic objectives might governments be trying to achieve? Try to think of objectives that all parties will have.

ANSWER

There are four economic objectives that are often seen as crucial:

- Full employment. Times are changing, and full employment (which means in practice a very low rate of unemployment) may no longer be attainable. Perhaps 'low unemployment' is a more realistic objective.
- A balance of payments. This means that what the country is buying in from abroad should not cost more than what the country sells abroad.
- Control of inflation. This means keeping price rises down to an acceptable level.

- Economic growth. So that the country as a whole becomes richer.

The relative importance given each of these four objectives will vary at different times. Any one party may when in government concentrate on one objective at the expense of others. Thus, some would argue that Harold Wilson's Labour government in 1969 concentrated on the country's balance of payments at the expense of controlling inflation. Some would argue that Margaret Thatcher's Conservative government from 1979 has concentrated on controlling inflation at the expense of full employment. What a government concentrates on will be determined by the general economic situation and by its own view of that situation.

Industrial relations are a crucial area in which management of the economy can meet success or failure. It is also true that the link between industrial relations and politics has a crucial influence on government views of economic objectives. To take one example, the Labour Party, with its strong trade union ties, would be more inclined to take action to alleviate unemployment (however much that may be a short-term palliative) than the Conservative Party.

So industrial relations affect the state's economic objectives and influence its success.

Activity

Read the newspapers and watch the news and current affairs programmes on television for a week. How often can you identify mentions of a link between industrial relations and the management of the economy?

The state as law-giver

One of the key functions of the state is to pass laws regulating the conduct of the people and organisations it controls. Britain, unlike the majority of countries, does not have a written constitution. Our laws have grown incrementally, bit by bit. This has had a major effect on industrial relations.

Many aspects of industrial relations, including our industrial system and the trade unions, existed before the state had passed any laws relating to them. Laws passed in the nineteenth century, before the mass of people were directly represented in Parliament, tended to restrict union activities. The unions were forced to campaign against such legislation and, in 1902, established their own party, the Labour Party, to help them do it.

Voluntarism

Over the years the trade unions developed the approach known as 'voluntarism'. 'Free collective bargaining' in negotiating (see Chapter 8) is the best-known feature of the voluntarist system, by which unions and employers are free to fix wages and working conditions between them. Voluntarism implies:

- the independence of industrial relations from government control;
- self-reliance of the trade unions – free to conduct their affairs as they see fit;
- a distrust of legislation.

The voluntary system is strongly rooted in the traditions of the trade union movement, but it is not an approach adopted solely by the unions. As an 'ideology' it has found easy acceptance with employers. Governments too have tended to accept the 'hands off' role that this ideology prescribes for them. When they have not, as during the period of the 1971 Industrial Relations Act, there was considerable evidence of connivance between unions and employers to preserve the voluntary character of their industrial relations arrangements.

Activity

What are the advantages and disadvantages for the unions and for managers of a 'voluntary' system? Try to think of advantages and disadvantages and ask yourself whether they apply to both sides, or just to one.

ANSWER

For the unions, voluntarism means that they have more freedom to conduct their affairs, there are few penalties when they break agreements and arrangements can be changed more easily. For the managers the benefits are exactly the same! Similarly with the disadvantages. The two sides have no recourse to anyone else if the agreements are broken; they have to rely on their own power and skill in all cases.

Since the mid 1960s, however, the concept of the abstention of the law from Britain's industrial relations has been a matter of intense debate.

Activity

Look at table 6, which details some of the legislation passed since 1970. Just at first glance, how many of the implications of voluntarism (p. 91) survive?

Table 6. Industrial relations legislation since 1970

1959
Terms and Conditions of Employment Act

1963, 1972
Contracts of Employment Acts

1965
Redundancy Payments Act

1970
Equal Pay Act

1971

Industrial Relations Act

1972
Industry Act

1973, 1981
Employment and Training Acts

1974
Health and Safety at Work Act

1974, 1976
Trade Union and Labour Relations Acts

1975
Sex Discrimination Act

1975, 1978
Employment Protection Acts

1976
Race Relations Act

1980
Employment Act

1982
Employment Act.

1984
Employment Act

ANSWER

It has been argued that there is very little of voluntarism remaining. We have already seen that through its role as dominant employer and via its management of the economy the state has a substantial controlling influence on the hard cash outcomes of collective bargaining. We noted in Chapter 3 that certain elements of the way the trade unions operate are controlled by law, and some of the laws in table 6 have added to that control. Whatever else we can see from the list of legislation since 1970 it is clear that, distrust it as they may, the parties to industrial relations are having to deal with an increasing amount of legislation.

It is still possible to argue that something of voluntarism remains. Those who make this case would point to four specific areas (although they would have to allow exceptions in each case):

● contractual freedom;
● freedom of bargaining arrangements;
● the non-legal nature of agreements;
● freedom to take industrial action.

Contractual freedom remains because most elements of the contract of employment are left to the two sides to agree. There are some legal minimum wages in a few small industries set by bodies known as wages councils. Some people have restrictions on their working hours built in by the law – lorry drivers and pilots, for example. There are a few legal requirements in all contracts of employment, on matters like notice periods on termination of the contract. In general, however, it is still the case in Britain, in contrast to many other countries, that there are very few legal restrictions on the terms of the contract of employment. Employers and employees may agree on any rate of pay, any hours of work and any amount of holidays that they wish.

Freedom of bargaining arrangements also remains. The law has restricted the way that agreements are made in very few particulars. Again the wages council industries are an exception. Otherwise managements can bargain with any union, any number of unions, or with none. There can be recourse to independent arbitrators when the negotiations get stuck – or not. Bargains can be made at national, regional or local level, or in each individual department. Management and unions are free to choose.

The non-legal nature of agreements is assumed. The negotiators can choose to make their agreements legally binding but very few if any do so. Indeed between 1971 and 1974, when the law was changed so that the assumption was that most agreements were legally binding unless otherwise stated, the vast majority of agreements included a clause stating specifically that they were binding in honour only.

Freedom of industrial action also remains. The legislation has reduced the type of industrial action that the union side can take without fear of penalty but has left most industrial action still exempt from claims for damages. The union cannot, in most cases, be sued for damages that the strike or go-slow or overtime ban has caused. And where the unions can be sued – where the action is not specifically directed against the strikers' own employer – the state has left it to the employer or a third party to take action. The state itself will not get involved.

Activity

Carry out your own opinion poll – ask ten people you know whether the law should be more involved in industrial relations. (If you really want to explore this topic see if you can argue against the views that each one has.)

We will examine this particular issue in more detail in Chapter 5. Some of the individual rights granted by the laws detailed in table 6 are explored in more depth in Chapter 6.

The state as provider of specialist services

The state provides many specialist services in the industrial relations area. These range from broad-range surveys and reports to detailed intervention in difficult situations.

Review

Why should the state provide specialist services in industrial relations? Think back over this chapter for a minute or two. Can you identify one overriding reason for this state provision?

ANSWER

A key part of the state's function is to manage the economy. If good industrial relations are vital to that management then it makes sense for the state to do what it can to foster good industrial relations. This is apart from any views about reducing the misery caused by industrial conflict or the rights of people at work.

The specialist services provided by the state come directly or indirectly. The direct services are the industrial tribunals or 'courts', the Central Arbitration Committee (CAC), the Advisory, Counciliation and Arbitration Service (ACAS) and a plethora of regular and occasional commissions, inquiries and committees. All these bodies play a direct part in industrial relations by intervening in situations which have become difficult.

There are also a host of indirect services: provided by the

Department of Employment, the National Economic Development-ment Council, the Manpower Services Commission and the commissions on equal rights for women and for minority ethnic groups.

One of the functions of the industrial relations expert in companies, or the trade union official, is to know which of these bodies to go to for which form of assistance.

Activity

If you want to know more about these bodies in any great detail, it's easy. Look up their address in the telephone directory and write to them. All of these organisations have simple booklets explaining their role and functions which they will be happy to send you.

What conclusions can we draw from all this? The state is a major employer, indeed by far *the* major employer: in this case the state is one of the two key parties in industrial relations. The state is required to manage the economy; therefore it is inevitably involved in influencing the atmosphere and often constraining the results of collective bargaining. The state makes the laws; in industrial relations as in other areas the state decides upon the legal framework. And the state provides specialist industrial relations services to those involved, to help them in difficult times.

The state sets the framework and is a major influence on industrial relations. It is crucial to our understanding of the subject.

Activity

Look at the industrial relations stories in the newspapers over the next three days. See if you can identify any way in which the state is involved and in which of the four cap-acities: as employer, as economic manager, as law-maker or as specialist.

5 | The law and collective bargaining

Compared to most countries, the law plays a small part in British industrial relations. Even in Britain, however, the law is an important element in the relationship between managements and trade unions and between managers and employees.* This chapter concentrates on the collective relationship: the way the law structures industrial relations at the management–union level.

The sources of the law

The first thing to establish is where the law comes from. Basically there are two different sources of law. These are, first, common law, or judge-made law; and second, statute law, or laws made by Parliament.

Common law in broad terms is that which has existed throughout history. There is no written constitution in Britain, but the courts have traditionally been prepared to insist on standards such as fairness and equity between individuals. Over time they have built up a body of cases or 'precedents' as they are called, which lay down principles that are followed by subsequent courts.

Statute law, by contrast, is legislation which has been passed by Parliament. Typically, it takes the form of an Act of Parliament, but it can also take other forms, such as Statutory Instruments. There is an enormous amount of legislation going through Parliament each year. In employment issues Parliament has been passing laws for over 150 years, but until the last two decades these have been few and far between. As we saw in Chapter 4 it is

*If you want to know more about the law in business, read a companion volume in the Pan Breakthrough series: *Practical Business Law* by Terry Price.

only recently that statute law has had any significant impact on industrial relations.

Industrial relations issues may be dealt with under either form of law. For example, a man who is injured at work may sue his employer (or take action at civil law, as the jargon goes) for the damage he has suffered. At the same time the health and safety inspector may, or may not, take the company to court for failing to obey the provisions of the Health and Safety at Work Act.

Industrial tribunals

The law governing industrial relations is to be found in both the common law and the statute law. Disputes arising out of statutory provisions which confer rights on individual workers normally are heard before industrial tribunals (ITs). These were established by Parliament in 1965. They consist of a lawyer-chairman and two 'sidesmen'; one from the employee's side and one from the management side. They all hear cases as individuals, not representatives, and the vast majority of their verdicts are unanimous. The sidesmen bring a knowledge of industry into the deliberations. The range of subjects covered by the ITs, their 'jurisdiction', is expanding all the time. It now covers the subjects noted in table 7. With a few exceptions these are issues which arise between employers and employees (or people who want to be or have just ceased to be employees). An individual who is unsatisfied with the decision at an industrial tribunal can appeal to the employment appeal tribunal, which is constituted along similar lines.

Table 7. Jurisdiction of industrial tribunals

Industrial tribunals cover claims in the following areas:

- Unfair dismissal.
- Redundancy payments.
- Consultation with recognised unions over redundancies and protection of employment.
- Statement of particulars of employment.
- Guaranteed pay.
- Suspension on medical grounds.

- Maternity rights (pay and return to work).
- Trade union membership and activities.
- Time off for union duties, activities, public duties, and to look for new work when redundant, and ante-natal care.
- Itemised pay statements.
- Written reasons for dismissal.
- Employee rights on insolvency.
- Equal pay.
- Sex discrimination.
- Race discrimination.
- Appeals against improvement and prohibition notices under Health and Safety at Work Act.
- Use of employer's premises for union ballots.
- Exclusion or expulsion from union.
- Appeals against industrial training levies.
- Docks and Harbours Act regulations.

Self-check

Why should industrial relations issues be dealt with in specialised tribunals and not in the ordinary courts?

ANSWER

The answer is that industrial relations issues need a faster, cheaper, more informal and more down-to-earth approach. If the dispute is about, say, the dismissal of an employee, and the remedy might be his or her re-engagement by the company, then it will not be sensible to wait some years for a hearing, or to make it so expensive that the employee cannot afford it, or so formal that he cannot put his own case, or so remote from his everyday experience that the issues are not understood. The industrial tribunal system aims to overcome these problems.

Codes of practice

Parliament has also recognised the different position of industrial relations in its use of 'codes of practice'. These are short, practical guidelines, usually issued with authority conferred by an Act of Parliament. The Secretary of State for Employment and ACAS have authority to issue such codes. They are not legally enforceable, but can be used as evidence in court. They operate in the same way as the Highway Code. It is not unlawful to ignore the Highway Code, but the police can argue in court that your failure to follow the code is convincing evidence of your committing an offence (such as dangerous driving).

There is a general code of practice on good industrial relations and there are other codes on such matters as disciplinary practices and procedures, disclosure of information, time-off facilities for shop stewards, picketing and the closed shop.

Activity

Write a sentence outlining some differences between an Act of Parliament and a code of practice.

ANSWER

An Act of Parliament is usually long, written in difficult legal terminology and has the full force of statute law. A code of practice is short, written in straightforward language and, whilst it can be quoted in evidence in a legal case, is intended rather to act as a guide.

Voluntarism and the law

We noted in Chapter 4 that Britain has had a long history of voluntarism in industrial relations.

Self-check

Write a sentence defining what we mean by voluntarism.

ANSWER

When you have written your definition look back to p. 91 and compare the definition there with yours.

A government discussion paper in 1981 summarised the traditional position of the law in industrial relations:

The way in which the law on industrial action has developed so far in this country has been characteristic of our industrial relations as a whole. Compared with most other countries there has traditionally been a minimum of legal interference and regulation. The conduct of our industrial relations is basically voluntary.

The government was arguing that despite the enormous amount of industrial relations law that has been passed in the last two decades (see p. 92 for a list) most of this has been aimed at improving protection for individual employees against arbitrary action on the part of managements. The collective relationships between managements and trade unions remain basically unfettered by law.

> ## Activity
>
> On the basis of your general knowledge, do you agree with the government's view that the conduct of collective bargaining is still basically voluntary? Do you think it should be?

ANSWER

Your answer to at least the second question takes us straight back to the values inherent in any discussion of industrial relations. There is no correct answer, only opinion. However, our opinions should be built on the basis of some facts. Remember that your answer so far will influence your view of what follows. We will examine the facts in the rest of this chapter so that we can ask ourselves the question again.

The status of trade unions

We noted the legal definitions of a trade union on p. 53. The significant effect of those definitions is that a combination of workers is regarded as a legal entity. The law regards the whole group of employees, the union, as a single body – capable of making contracts, owning property and so on. These bodies are legally required to keep proper accounts. Additional rights accrue in certain circumstances: these are, first, where the union is registered as independent and, second, where the union is recognised by the management of an organisation for negotiating and consultation purposes.

Unions can *register as independent* with the government-appointed certification officer. This officer keeps the rule books and accounts of all unions and can if requested issue certificates of independence to unions which satisfy certain criteria. These are that they are firmly established bodies independent (particularly financially) of the control and influence of employers with whom they deal.

Recognition, on the other hand, comes direct from the managers with whom the unions wish to negotiate. With recognition come additional legal rights for the union, and its members, that we will examine in a moment. First, however, the point has to be made that recognition of a trade union can be inferred from management action, as well as arising from a specific union agreement. Of course, if the management signs a recognition agreement the issue is clear-cut. However, should managers in an organisation refer continually to shop stewards to help them resolve problems then legally they will be deemed to have recognised the union even though no agreement has been signed.

The rights that unions can claim vary depending upon whether or not they are registered as independent and whether or not they are recognised. We will look at:

- the rights of members;
- the rights of union officials;
- rights to information and consultation.

The rights of members

Rights to join a trade union and take part in trade union activities are protected by law. It is unlawful for a manager to take any discriminatory action against an employee who wants to, or does, join an independent trade union. Nor can the management take discriminatory action against an employee who wants to take part in some union activity, such as attending a meeting, if that activity takes place outside working hours, at a tea or lunch break for example, or during working hours with a manager's consent.

It is possible for management to dismiss an employee who refuses to join a union, but only in particular cases where there is a union membership agreement with the union. These, known colloquially as 'closed shop' agreements, require everyone in a work area to be a union member. We will deal with them in detail in Chapter 7; here it suffices to say that in such cases a dismissal for not belonging to the union will be held to be fair only where a very substantial majority of the employees have been shown to be in favour of the closed shop.

The rights of union officials

The rights of union officials are more extensive than those of ordinary members. In addition to the right to take part in union activities, employee representatives at workplaces where the union is recognised can take time off for trade union duties. (The management must pay for this time at the normal rate.) We saw on p. 61 that many representatives spend a large proportion of their working hours on union business. Not all union business can be classified as 'duties': the law restricts that phrase to actions which are concerned directly with industrial relations issues at the workplace. Those union matters which are more general are excluded. We should note, however, that in practice many managements are more generous than they need to be under the strict letter of the law in allowing union representatives time off with pay.

|| *Activity*

|| Why should managers be more generous in the provision of time off or pay for time off than the law requires?

ANSWER

Your answer will depend upon your experience, and perhaps on your attitudes. If you are a cynic you might argue that it is because managements will see it as an easy way to curry favour with the union, or because it often costs more to work out how much money to deduct than just to pay a normal working week.

If you are more idealistic you might answer that it is in everyone's interest (and that includes the managers) if the representatives are professionally trained, and given the facilities to help resolve problems as soon as they arise.

Union representatives also have other rights. They are, for example, entitled to time off, with pay, for industrial relations training. Time off for such training, if it is approved by the representative's own union or the TUC, cannot lawfully be refused by management. Management may ask to see a syllabus, and can defer the time off if there are too many representatives off at once or if loss of the representatives would have a serious effect on the work. Otherwise they must allow the time off.

The representatives also have another advantage, though it is a recommendation in a code of practice and not part of the law. This is that they should not be dismissed until the management has notified their full-time official. This means that although they are subject to the same disciplinary rules as all other employees, there is an opportunity for an experienced union official to satisfy him or herself that the representative has not been victimised for undertaking the union job.

Rights to information and consultation

In addition to these, as it were, personal rights, the unions have other more general support from the law. They have the right to information to help them negotiate and, in certain circumstances, the right to be consulted. The right to disclosure of information is in effect severely restricted by a number of clauses which exclude, for example:

● information that would be difficult to obtain;
● information which might cause injury to the business if disclosed;
● information which was obtained in confidence.

The right of the union to be consulted arises in very specific circumstances where the union is independent and recognised. Managers must consult with properly appointed union safety representatives. They must consult with the union prior to declaring redundancies.

Self-check

We have been discussing the rights of individuals to join trade unions and take part in their activities; the rights of union officials; and rights to information and consultation. What could an individual do if he felt these rights had been refused by a management?

ANSWER

In practice the individual would probably contact a union's full-time official. What that individual or the official could do, if the management continued to refuse to grant these rights, is to take the matter to an industrial tribunal if it related to time off work for trade union duties. Where the complaint involved non-disclosure of information, the union would have to complain to ACAS, which, if it could not settle the dispute, would have to refer it to CAC for arbitration. The jurisdiction of the tribunals covers all these areas.

To summarise this section on the status of trade unions we can see that whilst the law accepts trade unions as corporate entities it places very few restrictions upon them. It does, however, give union members and officials some limited rights, designed to support collective bargaining between unions and management.

Strikes

We turn now to the position that the law takes when collective bargaining breaks down and there is a strike. The right to withdraw one's labour – or to strike, in everyday language – is seen widely in Britain as a right that is worth protecting. Parliament, including politicians from all political parties, has supported this right and made legislative provision for it to exist as a reality.

Activity

Take a few minutes to form and write down a sentence which starts: 'There should *not* be a right to strike because . . .' Then write a sentence which argues the opposite point of view: 'There *should* be a right to strike because . . .'

ANSWER

By now I will not have to point out the values inherent in your sentences. It is likely that if you were able to complete the first sentence you will have argued against a right to strike on the grounds of the damage that a strike inflicts. You could have written the second sentence, supporting a right to strike, on the grounds of Britain's obligation to uphold certain international declarations of human rights, or in terms of positive effects that strikes can have – forcing management to explain their actions or to avoid arbitrary whimsical decisions, for example. Most probably, however, your sentence has about it something of Winston Churchill's defence of democracy: of course, it's a pretty poor system; it's just that all the others are worse.

The alternative to having a right to strike is that management can take whatever action appeals to it on any issue without any concern for the consequences on the employees. Those employees are then left only with Hobson's choice: take it or leave it; accept whatever is done to them or leave the organisation and, very likely, become unemployed. In some less democratic countries this is precisely the situation that employees are in. Their working conditions are often scandalous. Other countries, indeed, even have forced labour.

In most advanced Western countries now employees are given the right to strike (though, naturally, the exact form of the right varies between nations). The British system, with no written constitution, finds it difficult to introduce a 'right to strike'. What we have instead is a 'negative right'. The unions are, in certain cases, protected from the possibility that they may be sued, and bankrupted, if strikes are called in their name.

This is done by the provision of a legal immunity. Union funds are protected (or 'immune') from civil proceedings taken against them in most strike situations. If the union, or more realistically an official acting in the name of the union, induces breaches of contract by calling a strike then the union cannot be sued for any damages caused by those broken contracts (though of course union officials are still subject to the criminal law).

The immunity depends upon the strike being called 'in contemplation or furtherance of a trade dispute'. This phrase is known in industrial relations circles as 'the golden formula'. In practice nearly all strikes have been covered by it. It is possible to conceive of strikes called for political purposes but these are extremely rare in Britain. Most union officials would argue that (in their perception at least) practically every strike is called in contemplation or furtherance of a trade dispute, but a recent Act of Parliament has redefined the golden formula to exclude certain cases, such as strikes called to support workers in other countries or taken to support fellow trade unionists in a totally separate company. The immunity is now restricted to disputes which occur between employees and management in a single organisation or in an associated organisation such as a different part of the same company. It excludes 'secondary action', as strikes called in sympathy with workers in dispute in other companies have come to be called.

As we saw in Chapter 1 most employees never use their right to strike. It is the ultimate sanction, understood by both sides in negotiations to be available to the unions as a final resort, but rarely used – although when it is used it gets a lot of publicity. Without the sanction in the background, however, the management would have no reason to negotiate, and the union no means of pressuring them to do so.

The legal position of a strike has in practice been of little importance compared to the power and determination of the two sides. Few employers are willing to prolong or exacerbate the bitterness which occurs during a strike by indulging in legal action against their employees or their unions.

Much more important than the legal position of the right to strike which underpins the negotiations is the legal status of the results of those negotiations – the collective agreement. Before we consider that, however, there is one aspect associated with strikes that creates a lot of argument. This is picketing.

Picketing

Picketing is a real issue in only a fraction of one per cent of cases, but it does catch a lot of media attention. Picketing is the act of gathering at a place of work to persuade people to support a strike. This may involve getting those people to join the strike, or just to stop deliveries to the workplace or some similar action. It creates controversy when it involves large numbers of pickets and they are seen to be intimidating. The classic examples occurred during the miners' strikes of 1972 and 1974 when they were able to stop deliveries of coal to power stations, the Grunwick dispute of 1978 and the *Stockport Messenger* dispute of 1983. There have been sporadic incidents of 'mass' picketing since.

Despite the controversy, the law has changed very little. Picketing has been restricted by recent Acts of Parliament to the place at which the picket actually works – or, if he is a trade union official, to the place at which his members work. Much more important are the Home Secretary's advice to the police on how they handle pickets, and the code of practice on picketing. Most of the obvious abuses of picketing are covered by the criminal law in any case; violence or physical intimidation are unlawful in any context. Probably this will continue to be an area where a few abuses get a lot of publicity, but the law is unable to provide a total solution.

Collective agreements

The precise nature of a contract of employment is unclear. Even the lawyers are still debating it. Important components of most individual contracts are, in practice, to be found in collective agreements – reached by unions and management as the result of negotiation.

Self-check

Why do most employees in Britain have major elements of their terms and conditions of work set by collective agreements?

ANSWER

The predominance of collective agreements reflects two essential facts, though there are some underlying facts which also have an impact. The two key facts are the convenience for all but the very smallest companies of having logical pay systems and arrangements, and the extensive influence of the trade unions in Britain. It is not unknown for unions to exist in organisations where individuals' pay is still determined by negotiations between the owner and each employee individually (union membership in such cases being almost an 'insurance policy' in cases of grievance). Nor is it unknown for large organisations to determine detailed salary structures for many employees with no union involvement. The general pattern, however, is that the trade unions are involved in the determination of pay structures through negotiation and collective agreements.

Underlying facts that help us to understand the predominance of collective agreements include the power position of the parties. Individual employees are rarely able to negotiate their terms and conditions of employment in practice. They are taken on by the organisation as, say, a warehouseman, on advertised pay rates. The company may have a warehouse wage structure with different rates depending on perhaps length of service, or age. In any case the employee is basically faced with 'take it or leave it'. If he is to influence the warehouseman's rate that he receives he can only do it once he has started work – through his union, i.e. collectively.

There are other elements too which explain the predominance of collective bargaining in the terms and conditions of most employees. We will only mention one other here, and that is the insistence in most circumstances that the agreements apply to all workers. On the management side this insistence stems from their need to maintain the logical relationship between groups and individuals; on the union side their determination to avoid non-union people being cheaper for the employer to hire. In any one factory or office there may be only, say, sixty per cent of employees who are union members – but the collective agreement will apply to all employees.

Overall the important point is that although only half the employees in Britain are union members, the terms and conditions of the vast majority of employees are determined in fact by collective agreements between unions and management.

Activity

Consider how important collective agreements are in determining your own pay and conditions. How are your increases determined? How does your holiday entitlement get changed? Is it done by agreements between the unions and management or between you and a particular manager – or is it part of one and part of the other? (If you are not in employment, ask someone you know.)

The legal status of this collective bargain is somewhat unclear, however. In line with the British tradition of voluntarism, agreements made between managements and trade unions are not legally enforceable. There was a short period in the early 1970s when the government of the day tried to ensure that union-management agreements could be held by the courts to be binding on the parties involved. But both unions and managements combined to ensure that they included in all agreements a clause that said something to the effect that 'This Is Not A Legally Enforceable Agreement.' (It was known, from its initials, as a Tina Lea clause!)

It seems that in practice there is no half-way house. Either you have a fully legalistic system like that in the United States of America, in which agreements between unions and managements are legal documents (often as large as two or three books the size of this one), drawn up by lawyers acting for each side; or you have a non-legalistic system. Agreements in Britain are non-legal, drawn up often on just two or three sheets of paper by the people who have to work under them.

That seems clear enough, and yet we said two paragraphs back that the situation was unclear. What haven't we mentioned? You will remember from p. 94 that the contract of employment is a contract like any other. That means it is legally enforceable. But we also said (p. 109) that most contracts of employment are determined by collective agreements – and they are *not* legally enforceable. If you are not sure where that leaves us, don't worry: the courts are not sure either! We do know that either the individual or the management can get the courts to enforce an individual contract; we do know that the courts will not enforce a collective agreement on the unions or on management. Some elements of the collective agreement are automatically included in the individual contract – pay, for example. Other elements we just do not know about.

In practice this uncertainty does not matter too much. The British tradition is to resolve these issues as far as possible without recourse to the law, so that at the workplace these delicate legal problems have very little impact.

The changing face of employment law

We have seen that the passing of law is one aspect of the state's involvement in industrial relations (Chapter 4). As such it is inevitably a political and value-laden activity. In Britain, unlike many other countries, there is a continuing political debate about the part the law should play in industrial relations.

Traditionally the law stayed out of industrial relations, particularly as far as collective bargaining was concerned. Over the last few years, however, the law has become progressively more involved: providing support to union members, encouraging collective bargaining and attempting to limit the power of the unions.

The main debate centres upon how the law can improve industrial relations. One side of this debate argues that the law should provide a generally supportive framework which encourages collective bargaining, but leaves the parties concerned free to get on with it. After all, it is said, it is the managers and workforce involved who have to live with the results. Furthermore, history shows that it is difficult to enforce the law on hundreds of thousands of union members who will not accept it. History also shows that in recent times the most acrimonious disputes have been *about* the law rather then resolved by it. So, it is argued, the law should stay out.

The alternative argument is that despite the law staying out of industrial relations the parties have not reformed themselves. Perhaps the law should be more involved in deciding who should join which unions, when employers should recognise them, when they should negotiate and on what subjects, and in restricting the right to strike. The fact that such legal interventions have been less than successful in the past, or that they are contentious, is no reason for rejecting the good that the law can do.

Activity

Think about this debate, discuss it with colleagues. Which side are you on?

6 | Individuals and employment law

Whilst the law has in general stayed out of the collective side of industrial relations, at least until recently, it has been much more active in the relationship between individuals and their employers.

The objective of this chapter is not to turn you into a labour lawyer. In fact we will avoid using 'legalese'. What we will try to do is explain what employment legislation means for managers and individuals at work.

In broad terms the legislation provides a series of 'protections' for individual employees (see table 8). They are extensive and some of them are based on several pieces of legislation (see table 6). To go through every Act of Parliament, some of which amend previous Acts of Parliament, would be complicated and unnecessary. So we will follow the course of an employment relationship, starting when the company decides to take on a new employee and taking it through to dismissal or resignation, looking at all the law that applies at each stage. We will look at what the law requires before an employee is taken on, what legislation applies when the employee joins a company, what the law means during employment and what it means on termination of the contract.

Table 8. Legal protection for employees

Employees have rights:

- not to be discriminated against on grounds of sex or married status;
- not to be discriminated against on racial grounds;
- not to be discriminated against on grounds of trade union membership or activities;
- to a written statement of the main terms and conditions of their employment;
- to safe working conditions;

- to full payment as agreed;
- to various forms of assistance if made redundant;
- to time off for public duties;
- not to be dismissed for reason of pregnancy;
- to time off for ante-natal care;
- to maternity pay;
- to return to work following a confinement;
- to proper notice of dismissal;
- to written reasons when dismissed;
- not to be unfairly dismissed.

All may be subject to meeting specific requirements.

Before joining

When an employing organisation requires new staff it is in general free to take whatever steps it feels appropriate to recruit them. There are now, however, a limited number of restrictions imposed by law; mostly with the intention of preventing sexual and racial discrimination. It is unlawful to discriminate in the arrangements that are made to recruit staff.

Activity

How might a manager discriminate in the arrangements made (or methods used) to recruit a new member of staff?

ANSWER

Managers have found a variety of ways to discriminate. Most of them occur in advertisements, application forms, interviews and on selection.

In *advertisements* it is illegal to show an intention to discriminate. So words like 'waitress' – which shows a clear intention to choose a woman – or 'English receptionist' – which may show an intention to exclude black applicants – are not allowed.

Similar rules apply in *application forms*. Not only must any words which show evidence of intent to discriminate be avoided; but so must any discriminating questions. Asking women whether they intend to stop work to have a family, for example, is discriminatory, because men would not be asked the same question.

Questions are also asked at *interviews*, and here again the manager involved must be careful not even to appear to discriminate. Managers are often advised nowadays to keep succinct, but clear, notes on the candidates as they interview them so that when the *selection* is made they can justify their decision if a disappointed candidate should make a claim of discrimination to an industrial tribunal.

Non-discrimination laws are the most important to apply during the recruitment procedures, but not the only ones. There is legislation which encourages the hiring of a percentage of registered disabled employees and another law which says that criminal convictions must be disregarded in the appointment process after a certain amount of time.

For most companies these limitations on recruitment are hardly onerous. 'It's always our objective to find the best person for the job', one manager told me, 'not just irrespective of sex or colour, but irrespective of everything except whether they can do the job.' With that objective, carried out rationally, managers will find that the law imposes no limits upon their ability to advertise, recruit and select whom they want.

On joining

Conditions agreed at the start of employment between the individual and the managers who represent the organisation influence the relationship from then on. In general the law leaves the parties substantially free to agree whatever terms they choose. There are, of course, restrictions on potential discrimination; there are restrictions on pay comparability, in that men and women doing the same job must not be on different pay scales; and there are restrictions on the employment of women and young persons in certain occupations and at night. Unlike many other countries, Britain has with only a few exceptions no legal minimum wage, no automatic rights to holidays and very restricted requirements for providing or, more accurately, passing on certain state sickness and pension provisions. The contractual relationship is determined mainly by the agreement between the parties.

A contract exists as soon as the employee starts work. Even if there is no written documentation the courts and tribunals are able to 'infer' contractual details from the behaviour of the parties. This means that if the company contrives to provide work and pay and the employee continues to do the one and accept the other then both sides are deemed to be bound by a contract of employment.

The contract of employment

The relationship between the individual and his employing organisation is structured by the contract of employment. Like all contracts, it has three components. Where would you look for evidence of a contract of sale between, for instance, the purchaser and seller of a motorbike? In the *written documents* of course: the bill of sale and perhaps the hire purchase agreement. What if the seller then said, 'Ah, I know I said you could ride it away for £100 and so you can; however, the lights and brakes will cost you another £50'? Well, if the seller persisted the purchaser could go to court: and the court would say that the law insists that if it's sold as a motorbike, it must be 'roadworthy', which means having lights and brakes. These are *minimum legal requirements*. And there are still other requirements. What if the bike was delivered with square wheels? The law can help here too. The courts would say that there are *implied terms*, assumptions shared by most people who know about motorbikes; that, in this case, they have round wheels.

These same three elements are present in all contracts. They have, in general, this order of priority:

1 minimum legal requirements;
2 written terms;
3 implied terms.

In other words the implied terms are overridden by written terms, but if the written terms and the legal requirements are at odds then the legal requirements take precedence. These three elements, with the same order of priority, are also found in contracts of employment.

The minimum legal requirements in a contract of employment are, in line with the tradition of voluntarism, very limited. With the exception of a few occupations, such as airline pilots and heavy-goods vehicle drivers, most people are free to agree contracts to work for as long as they want, and for as little money as they like. There are no limitations in law. The main legal limitations are on written information that has to be given, on periods of notice for termination of the contract, and on safety. Employees are also entitled to 'guarantee payments' when their company cannot provide them with work on a particular day, to statutory sick pay and, in a few specific industries, to a minimum wage agreed by that industry's 'wages council'. (Wages councils are meetings of employers, union and an independent group, appointed by the state to establish minimum wage levels for the industry.)

The written documents can be very varied indeed. They include any written details of the agreement between the individual and the employing organisation.

Activity

What written documents could include details of the contract of employment? Think of your own work if you are in employment: what is written down about your job and the remuneration you get for it? What documents can you find that in?

ANSWER

The range is enormous. Some people have no written details at all; but if they are in work they still have a contract of employment. In other cases you might find details of the contract in:

- a letter of appointment;
- union agreements;
- works rules;
- job descriptions;
- departmental notices;
- pension rules;

and a host of other places – anywhere, in short, that tells you what is required in the job, and what you receive for doing it.

There is now a requirement that by the time employees have been in employment for thirteen weeks they must be given a *written statement of the main terms and conditions of employment*. This can include anything but must at least cover the following points:

- names of employer and employee;
- date employment began, and whether any previous service is continuous;
- job title (a job description is not required);
- rate of remuneration or method of calculating it (remuneration includes *all* forms of pay);
- whether pay is weekly, monthly or at some other interval;
- hours of work and normal working hours;
- entitlement to annual holidays, holiday pay and public holidays;
- conditions relating to sickness, injury and sick pay;
- conditions relating to pension;
- length of notice the employee is obliged to give and entitled to receive (this may exceed the statutory minimum but cannot be less);
- disciplinary rules, and the person to whom the employee can appeal against any disciplinary decision;
- name of the person who will deal with grievances and the procedure to be followed.

The written statement can merely tell the employee where to find some of this information (in, for example, a union – management agreement) provided that the information is readily accessible to the employee.

The implied terms, the third component of the contract, are inevitably more difficult to define. To understand the meaning of these terms think what might happen if research scientists were asked to sweep the floor. Even if there was no written statement of the terms of employment they could refuse, arguing that everyone would accept that it was not part of a research scientist's job to sweep floors. Of course most cases are less clear than this. That is why in an increasing number of cases employers are putting more and more details of the contract of employment into the written terms.

In reality the new employee does not sit down with the manager and negotiate the terms and conditions that make up the contract of employment. What happens is that a job vacancy is made known. The type of job creates very clear expectations about the basic terms and conditions that may be applicable.

Activity

Match the jobs in column *A* with the salaries in column *B* and the other elements of terms and conditions in column *C*:

A	B	C
Sales director	£140 per week	long holidays
Painter and decorator	£15,000 per year	large company car
Secretary	£25,000 per year	free overalls
Van driver	£6,000 per year	luncheon vouchers
College lecturer	£180 per week	use of vehicle

ANSWER

Your chart should look like this:

A	B	C
Sales director	£25,000 per year	large company car
Painter and decorator	£180 per week	free overalls
Secretary	£6,000 per year	luncheon vouchers
Van driver	£140 per week	use of vehicle
College lecturer	£15,000 per year	long holidays

The point of the activity is that most of us with experience of industry will have found that chart relatively easy to amend accurately. So if, to take one example, the job that is advertised is 'secretary', an applicant will know that they are unlikely to be offered very long holidays or £15,000 per year.

Furthermore, not only is the range of options limited by expectations but limits are also imposed by the company's pay structures and by trade union agreements. In general the organisation will want to fit new employees into its pay structure at a point that is fair to other employees. Agreements that it may have with trade unions will determine the pay and conditions applicable to any particular post in some detail.

In practice therefore 'negotiation' of the contract often amounts to a 'take it or leave it' exercise. The 'agreement' that the lawyers look for as crucial to bringing the contract into force is a legal abstraction; reality is usually acceptance of Hobson's choice.

Other legal provisions

Other legal provisions on joining are hardly more onerous than the requirement to give written details of the contract. There should be a proper induction of the employee explaining the job that has to be done and the rules that operate. In itself this is not a legal requirement but may avoid problems with disciplinary issues or unfair dismissal (which we will examine later on in this chapter). There should also be a thorough explanation of the safety rules and procedures (and we will also discuss this issue in more detail later). However, and this is a point we will make again in relation to the employment law that applies to individuals, these are things that should be done as a matter of good management practice even if no law applied.

The law during employment

So our individual has been taken on as an employee. What does the law require now? There are some general implied terms which can be drawn from the common law, which are part of the implied terms of the contract of employment. We will also need to be aware of the way the contract is changed. Then we will look at the specific issues of discrimination, on grounds of sex, race or trade union membership, time-off provisions, maternity provisions and health and safety law.

Common law terms

The common law obligations imposed on managers and employees arise from the notions of fair treatment and faithful service. So managements are expected to pay full remuneration, to ensure safety, not to ask employees to break the law and to provide reasonable working conditions. Employees are expected to work properly and to take reasonable care to avoid damage or injury (to themselves or anything or anyone else). They are expected to obey all lawful and reasonable instructions and rules and not to damage their company's interest by, for example, disclosing confidential information. In most cases these common law duties are so much a part of our thinking that they are taken for granted. When disputes do occur they tend to be about whether instructions are 'reasonable' (to take one typical instance); there is rarely any disagreement about the fact that employees *should* obey reasonable instructions.

Changes to the contract

Changes are made to a contract of employment by agreement between the parties. A large number of these changes are made through management – union agreements. The trade unions are not parties to individual contracts but the law assumes that the management, in recognising the unions for negotiating purposes, and the employees, by working in areas covered by the unions, are, as it were, automatically agreeing that the result of management–union negotiations will change the contract.

Other changes, particularly changes in working practices or in the physical conditions of work, are often made without any formal agreement with employees directly or with their representatives.

Self-check

Think about the discussions so far. How might a change to the contract of employment occur if there is no formal agreement?

ANSWER

Like the 'agreement' at the start of the contractual relationship, it can be inferred from the behaviour of the parties. If managers make a change to the way work is carried out, or move the

location at which employees work, then as long as the latter
continue to do the work and to receive pay for it they can be held
to have 'agreed' to the change. Equally, if managers continue to
pay factory workers, say, who insist on stopping work fifteen
minutes early each day to 'clean up' that clean-up time can be
assumed to be part of the agreed contract of employment.

Problems arise when changes made to the contract are not
clearly notified and agreed. This is especially so where changes
are to the implied terms and, by their nature, the implied terms
are open to different interpretations. The situation looks very
confused to American and European experts visiting Britain:
their contracts are all in writing, voluminous 'books' detailing all
the terms. But, in practice, the British system of contracts of
employment does work and only a tiny percentage of cases in
which the contract is changed cause any difficulty.

Discrimination

We have already talked briefly about discrimination in the
recruitment and selection process. Laws against discrimination
also apply throughout the employment relationship. Before
examining these in more detail, we will need a clearer understanding of what the law means by 'discrimination'. There are
two forms of discrimination: direct and indirect.

Activity

Assume that you are a manager considering the promotion
of one of twenty individuals to a supervisory job and that
you have decided that you do *not* want one of the ten
woman to get the job. Apart from directly restricting
applications for the job to the men, how might you phrase a
notice inviting applications for the job so that it in fact goes
to a man?

ANSWER

You may have been extremely imaginative in your reply, but
what you have probably suggested is some requirement that the
women would find it difficult to meet. You might, for example,

have suggested that all applicants must be at least six feet tall. This is an example of what the law calls indirect discrimination. It applies in cases of racial discrimination in exactly the same way.

It is unlawful to discriminate by providing less favourable opportunities for promotion, or training; or worse facilities, benefits or services. It is unlawful to do this:

● *directly* by treating one person less favourably than another on grounds of sex or race;
● *indirectly* by applying a requirement which applies to all, but which means that a smaller proportion of one race or sex can meet it, unless the requirement is justifiable in any case, or is not to the detriment of any race or sex.

The word 'justifiable' in that definition of indirect discrimination applies to requirements for physical ability in certain jobs (such as firemen), or the requirement of decency. In practice such 'justifiable' discrimination is very limited. Discrimination can also be lawful in cases where a 'genuine occupational qualification' applies: Chinese waitress in a Chinese restaurant, or women in a dramatic production, for example.

A third form of unlawful discrimination is that against trade union members. Managers must not prevent employees from being union members, nor, as we saw in the previous chapter, should they prevent them from taking part in the activities of their union. It is unlawful to penalise the employees in any way for being union members or being involved with union activities. So any manager who offers less attractive or less remunerative work to union members, or refuses to promote them, can be taken to an industrial tribunal. Furthermore, if the manager goes a step further, and dismisses anyone for being a union member, that will be an automatic unfair dismissal.

Time off

Employees are entitled to appropriate time off to take part in union activities. We noted in the previous chapter that union representatives have rights to time off (with pay) for trade union duties and training, and we shall see that safety representatives are also entitled to time off to perform their duties and to receive training. Pregnant women have a right to time off for ante-natal care. And there are yet other categories of people with a legal entitlement to take time off work. Time off in cases of redundancy will be examined when we cover that topic at the end of the chapter.

The other major entitlement is for time off to perform *public duties*. Those who do so, including people carrying out jury service, for example, generally receive some expenses from the public body concerned so there is no legal requirement for the organisation to pay for the time the employee has off – although most make up the employee's pay to what it would have been had they not performed the public duty.

'Reasonable' time off (which means not too much, or not at inconvenient times) must be allowed for activities carried out as:

- a justice of the peace;
- a member of a local authority;
- a member of any statutory tribunal;
- a member of a regional health authority or area health authority;
- a member of the managing or governing body of a local-authority-maintained educational establishment;
- a member of a water authority.

Maternity provisions

Pregnant employees can now claim four rights under the law: the right not to be dismissed, the right to time off for ante-natal care, the right to maternity pay and the right to return to work after confinement. We will look at each of these in turn.

The right not to be dismissed because she is pregnant applies to all women who have worked full-time for an organisation for one year or more. The law says that the woman can be dismissed if she is incapable of doing her job adequately or if, because of health and safety or other legal provisions, there would be a breach of some other law if she contrived to work. Even in these cases there is a requirement that the management should check whether there might not be other work that would be suitable, and if there is, to offer that rather than dismiss.

Time off for ante-natal care is any woman's entitlement as long as she continues to work. Any such time off must be paid for at the normal rate.

Maternity pay must be given to all pregnant women when they stop work to have the baby, provided that they meet a series of conditions. To qualify a woman must:

- have worked full-time for the organisation for at least two years;
- work up to at least the eleventh week before the expected date of confinement; and
- inform her manager at least 21 days before she stops work.

Maternity pay works out at almost a normal week's pay for six weeks after the woman stops work. The employer receives the money back from the government's maternity pay fund.

The right to return to work is subject to the same conditions as maternity pay. In addition the woman not only has to inform her manager that she is leaving work but also that she intends to come back. The woman has up to 29 weeks after the expected date of confinement in which she can return to work. She decides if and when she wants to start work again, but she has to give 21 days notice of her intention to return. The company can ask her to clarify her intentions, in writing, once 49 days following the expected date of confinement have passed. When the woman has asked to return to work the employer can delay it for up to four weeks. Also the woman can, if she is ill, extend the 29 week limit by four weeks.

Self-check

> Assuming a woman has worked full-time for an organisation for two years or more, and fulfils all the legal requirements, which is the maximum period that she could be off work and still have a legal right to return?

ANSWER

It is probably around 45 weeks: eleven weeks before the expected date of confinement and 29 weeks after the actual date plus four weeks' delay plus perhaps a week or so's difference between the expected and actual date of confinement.

Health and safety at work

An increasingly important area of legislation concerns health and safety at work. This is one area where both civil law and criminal law have substantial impact.

There has always been a common law duty on all 'masters' (now represented by managers) to take reasonable care of their 'servants' (or employees). Where the employer fails to fulfil that duty, and the employee is injured or made ill, the employer can be taken to court and compensation will be awarded.

Over the years this common law duty has been supplemented by successive Acts of Parliament. These have laid down a series of minimum standards in agriculture, mines and quarries, factories, offices, shops and railways. Examples of the kind of standards laid down are given in table 9.

Table 9. Examples of minimum standards required by the Offices, Shops and Railway Premises Act 1963

Overcrowding
Minimum of 40 square feet of floor space each; where the ceiling is lower than 10 feet, at least 400 cubic feet per person must be allowed. (Ignore furniture, fittings, etc. when measuring.)

Temperature
After the first hour, temperature should be at least 16°C (60.8°F) where the work does not involve 'severe physical effort'.

Methods of heating likely to cause injuries or offensive fumes are prohibited.

A thermometer must be placed in a conspicuous place on each floor.

Toilets
Regulations lay down a scale of how many closets must be provided for each sex:

1–15 people	1 closet
16–30 people	2
31–50 people	3
51–75 people	4
76–100 people	5

over 100 people   5 – with an additional closet for every 25 persons in
                       excess of 100

First aid
A first aid box must be provided for the use of all employees. An
additional box must be provided for every 150 persons.

It was decided, however, that not only was it possible for
companies to meet all these standards and still have a dangerous
workplace, but that many millions of employees were not
covered by them.

In 1974 therefore Parliament introduced, with all-party support the Health and Safety at Work, etc. Act (HASAWA). This
put a duty on *every employing organisation* 'to ensure so far as is
reasonably practicable, the health, safety and welfare at work of
all employees'. This general duty was supplemented by several
specific duties, requiring management:

● To provide and maintain plant and systems of work that are, so
  far as is reasonably practicable, safe and without risk to health.
● To ensure that arrangements in connection with the use,
  handling, storage and transport of articles and substances are
  safe and healthy, so far as is reasonably practicable.
● To provide such information, training and supervision as is
  considered necessary to ensure the health and safety at work of
  the employees, so far as is reasonably practicable.
● To maintain safe and healthy conditions at any place of work
  which is under the employer's control; and to maintain safe
  and risk-free access and exits from the workplace (so far as is
  reasonably practicable).
● To provide and maintain a working environment which is free
  from risk to health, and safe, so far as is reasonably practicable; with adequate facilities for the welfare at work of the
  employees.

The key phrase is 'so far as is reasonably practicable'. What
does it mean? It is intended to be a statement that will vary with
circumstances, so there can be no blanket answer. We know,
from legal cases, that just because something is physically possible the courts will not necessarily consider it to be reasonably
practicable. We also know that just because something will cost a

lot of money to make safe that does not necessarily mean it is *not* reasonably practicable. The courts will weigh the extent and likelihood of the possible danger against the cost and time involved in taking precautions. If the danger is high they will expect the management to be prepared to put a lot of time and money into reducing it; but if the danger is remote that would not be reasonable.

Activity

Think of a dangerous situation. You may know of one at work or you may be able to imagine one. What action do you think would be 'reasonably practicable' as a precaution?

In addition to the duties we have noted so far the Health and Safety at Work Act includes one unusual and interesting requirement. This is that all work organisations must have a *safety policy* and that in all but the smallest the policy should be written down and published to managers and other employees. The safety policy should consist of:

- a general statement of intent;
- a statement of the way the organisation will carry out that intent, with details of who is responsible for what;
- details of the arrangements for carrying out the policy – which might well vary from area to area within the workplace.

Self-check

Look back to our discussion of the differences between the civil law and criminal law (p. 98). Bearing in mind that discussion and the points made above write down two ways in which the Health and Safety at Work Act differs from the common law rights and two ways in which it differs from previous safety laws.

ANSWER

The Health and Safety at Work Act is part of the criminal law, but its general duties look very like the civil law provisions.

Because they have been translated into the criminal law, however, it means that:

- there is a 'policing force' (called the Health and Safety Inspectorate) set up to ensure that it is followed and to take action against anyone who breaks it;
- there is no requirement to wait for an injury to occur before action can be taken. Companies whose premises are unsafe, for example, can end up before a court even if there has been no accident (yet);
- penalties are imposed for not following the law. Under civil law only compensation is awarded.

The Health and Safety at Work Act also differs from previous safety laws in that:

- everyone at work is covered. There are no exceptions;
- no minimum standards are laid down. The duties are to keep things and people safe, and details may vary according to circumstances;
- the emphasis is on the provision of safe systems and people working safely, rather than on safe equipment.

The Health and Safety at Work Act is not intended to be the last word on safety, replacing all other safety laws. The Act set up the Health and Safety Commission with representatives from employing organisations, trade unions and others. The commission's duties include producing new codes of practice, and submitting proposals for amending legislation and introducing new safety regulations. We can confidently predict that this is one area at least where legislation will increase.

Health and Safety Inspectorate The Commission's other duties include overseeing the work of the Health and Safety Inpsectorate. The inspectors have extensive authority. They can enter premises without the owner's approval (at reasonable times), they can examine anything, take things away, go through papers, obtain information from anyone and they can issue 'improvement notices', requiring a company to put some breach of the law right, and 'prohibition notices', which prevent an activity being carried out unless some fault is remedied. As the law provides, in serious cases, for penalties in the courts including imprisonment and/or unlimited fines, it is clear that the inspectors have very real powers.

So far we have spoken only of the effect of HASAWA on managers. But, of course, *employees* can also be responsible for unsafe practices. This law also puts obligations on every employee. These are:

- to take reasonable care for the safety of themselves, their workmates and anyone else they may affect;
- to cooperate with their managers in safety matters;
- not to interfere with or misuse safety equipment provided under any of the legislation.

In addition to employers and employees the Act contains important provisions relating to trade unions. Where they have been recognised by management they are given the right to appoint *safety representatives* and, where the representatives request it, to set up a *safety committee*. The commission has issued guidance on representatives and committees.

The representatives' functions are to provide an internal check upon and support for management in ensuring safety. They can check on complaints from their members, check the measures management are taking and investigate potential dangers and the causes of accidents that have occurred. They should work with management to carry out regular inspections, to attend the safety committee and to make representations to management about the safety of the workplace.

Employees acting as safety representatives are specifically protected from legal action against them for anything said or done as a representative. (They are still required to fulfil the duties of employees.) This exemption was probably included in the Act because, otherwise, very few employees would have accepted the job, but it also helps to emphasise the responsibility of management to evaluate and act upon the advice they receive.

Like shop stewards or other employee representatives, safety representatives have rights to paid time off work to carry out their duties and to attend training courses. The TUC has mounted a massive safety representatives' training programme. Despite many fears and concerns in the early days, the system seems to be working well in most workplaces.

The safety committees are the forum in which management and representatives can together assess what needs to be done, ensure that it is done and monitor the results. They are the formal, regular, most wide-ranging expression of what should be a continuing liaison between management and safety representatives.

The law requires the management of an organisation to accept safety representatives and set up safety committees where a trade union is recognised and asks for these rights. There are also many situations in which either no union is recognised, or the union has not asked, in which the company still encourages the appointment of representatives and sets up safety committees. As always, employing organisations are free to do more than the law requires; and many non-union companies see a value in having their own employee safety representatives and safety committees.

Review

The Bone Company warehouse is in the Midlands. The company has a proper safety policy and a safety committee is in operation. Safety shoes have been issued to all employees but only some of them wear the shoes. It has been the practice to 'roll' heavy pieces on to the forks of the forklift trucks but the safety committee has found out that this is regarded as dangerous by the inspectorate. The safety representatives had a discussion with the warehouse manager about this and have agreed to continue the practice for the time being but to review it at the next committee meeting. Last week one of the warehouse supervisors ordered Harry Jones to 'roll' a piece out but he refused, saying it was unsafe. The supervisor repeated his order and Harry, being rather angry, rolled the piece too hard and crashed it on to the foot of Bob Price, one of his workmates. Bob was not wearing safety shoes and his foot was badly injured. After he had been taken to hospital the safety inspector was called in. Whom would the inspector hold responsible?

ANSWER

The law, and the inspector, would take the common-sense view that in this case (as in so many) responsibility is shared. Clearly the warehouse manager has not ensured that there are safe systems of work. The supervisor too is at fault: not only did the supervisor order Harry to carry out an unsafe practice but that supervisor, or perhaps all the supervisors, were at fault in not ensuring that the warehouse workers wore their safety shoes. Harry has some excuse, in that he was carrying out a direct order and that he had challenged it on the grounds of safety. The inspectors understand that employees cannot continue to refuse to obey direct orders. But he had then let his temper cause an accident. Even Bob Price is partly at fault: because he should have been wearing his protective shoes. Finally, although the inspector might think that the safety representatives were at fault in accepting the continuation of an unsafe practice you will remember that this is one group which cannot be taken to court.

Termination of the contract

All contracts of employment are terminated eventually. In some circumstances, such as the death or retirement of the employee, there is very little legislative involvement. In other cases a fixed-term contract expires and is not renewed, or the employee resigns, because he or she has found a better job or for some other reasons. These situations are uncontentious and provided that proper notice is given and administrative details are carried out correctly they go through without comment or concern. Those cases form the great majority of terminations.

Problems arise over cases of dismissal of the employee. (In law the word 'dismissal' includes cases where the management's action has been such that it has indicated an intention not to be bound by the contract and so the employee has resigned – this is called 'constructive dismissal'.)

Unfair dismissal

Around 30,000 applications for unfair dismissal are filed each year. Of these approximately one third are withdrawn at an early stage as being unlikely to succeed; one third are 'settled out of court' (usually with a payment of compensation); and one third go to an industrial tribunal hearing. In approximately one quarter of the tribunal hearings (that is, roughly one twelfth of the applications) the employee wins his case, and the dismissal is found to be unfair.

Compensation in the tribunals can, in theory, amount to many thousands of pounds, but in practice most unfairly dismissed employees receive only a few hundred pounds. This is because the sums awarded are largely related to length of service with the particular organisation which unfairly dismissed the employee and to compensation for loss of earnings. If the employee was not employed by that company for very long (and that is so in the majority of cases), or has found a job again fairly swiftly, then compensation will be correspondingly small. Compensation is not related to how unfair the dismissal was.

Activity

Only a small number of cases are won each year, and very limited sums of compensation are generally awarded, so what are the benefits of this piece of legislation? Try to think of at least two potential benefits.

ANSWER

The legislation and the results outlined above have been criticised, by the trade unions especially, for being weak, but they have achieved the following benefits:

- Companies have in general clarified their procedures and policies in the years since the unfair dismissal provisions were introduced.
- Companies and those who advise them on one side, and trade union members on the other, now have an independent third party to whom they can turn in contentious cases: the choice is no longer just 'strike or accept it'.

- For those people involved in the cases even the small numbers appear to be justifiable. If there was only one case, and it was yours, it would seem important and worthwhile to you.
- Many aggrieved employees go to tribunals in order to prove that their dismissal was wrong. The compensation is much less central to their motives, so they are less concerned if it is a small amount.
- Overall there seems little doubt that the effects of the legislation on management thinking are significant. Whatever the likelihood of an employee winning his case and whatever the cost involved, managers do not want to get taken to tribunals. So the law has made them more careful.

Before we examine the unfair dismissal requirements we need to note the distinction between unfair and wrongful dismissal, and the groups of employees who cannot claim unfair dismissal.

Wrongful dismissal applies to any dismissal which is in breach of contractually agreed or legally required terms. The termination of a contract (with due notice) is not a breach of it; all employment contracts terminate sooner or later. And we have seen that the legal requirements are extremely limited. In practice the phrase 'wrongful dismissal' applies to cases in which the employee has not been given proper notice. The employee is entitled to sue for compensation to cover what he or she has lost during the period in which the notice would have applied. At the moment this action is taken through the civil courts, though there is provision to transfer these cases to industrial tribunals in the future. We will look in detail at 'unfair' dismissals in a moment.

Not everyone can claim unfair dismissal. The law excludes three main groups and several smaller categories from this protection. The three main groups excluded are:

- employees with insufficient service; they have to have worked for the same organisation for at least one year, or at least two years if the company employs twenty or less;
- employees past normal retiring age;
- part-time workers: those who work less than sixteen hours per week or, if they have worked there for five years or more, those who work less than eight hours.

Other exclusions cover such groups as spouses of the owner of the business, share fishermen, the armed services and police, and certain cases of individuals who are on strike.

These groups are excluded. What about those who *can* claim unfair dismissal? What is it that the law requires managers to do? The obvious answer – not to dismiss employees unfairly – is accurate but unhelpful. How are managers to know what is unfair? Well, common sense and experience are important, and we can also get some guidance from the cases that have been considered.

First, the manager has to be sure that the *reason for dismissal* is a fair one. Generally this means that the dismissal has to be because of:

- the employee's misconduct;
- a lack of capability on the part of the employee to do the job; or
- redundancy – in other words there is no longer a job for the employee to do.

There are a few other reasons which can be held to be fair but the vast majority of cases fall under one of these three headings. Some reasons – race and sex discrimination and trade union membership or activities – are specifically held to be *inadmissible reasons*.

Even if the manager is sure that the dismissal is for one of the three main reasons there is still a requirement that dismissal is *reasonable in the circumstances*.

Activity

Take the simple case of theft. Clearly this falls under the fair reason of misconduct. If you were the manager would you dismiss the employee if what had been stolen was:

- a paperclip?
- a typewriter ribbon?
- several notebooks and some pens?
- a calculator?
- an old typewriter?
- the petty cash box with £100 in it?

ANSWER

It depends on the circumstances. Most of us would not dismiss someone for stealing a paperclip –and the tribunals would certainly find such a dismissal unfair. Other cases might depend on factors such as: how much loyal service the employee had; whether they worked in a security-conscious area; whether they were in a position of trust; whether lots of other things had been stolen from that department. In other words, the surrounding facts have to be taken into account. Let us examine some of the circumstances tribunals expect to be considered in each of the three mains areas.

Misconduct cases In these cases the Tribunals expect:

- that managers will have given employees full warning of the consequences of breaches of the rules and to have repeated that in specific cases for all but the most serious misconduct;
- that the employee concerned will have an opportunity to explain their side of the story before any decision to dismiss is taken and will, if so desired, have been allowed to be accompanied to any such hearing by a colleague or representative;
- that action is taken through a proper disciplinary procedure, with a right of appeal to a higher level of management.

Cases of lack of capability can come in two forms: either the employee is too ill to be able to perform the job, or is perfectly fit but simply cannot do the work. In cases of long absence from work due to ill health the tribunals are not keen to see employees dismissed but will accept it if:

- the needs of the business are such that the position must be filled;
- the employee's chances of recovery and future prospects have been examined – with the individual if possible;
- the manager has looked at alternatives (shorter hours, changed rosters, different work); and
- the individual has been warned in due time of the possibility of dismissal.

In cases of lack of skill or poor performance the tribunals expect the following:

- proof: not proved 'beyond reasonable doubt' as in a criminal court, but some clear evidence that the employee cannot do the job;
- help from management: explaining what is required to the employee, training, if appropriate, proper supervision;
- warnings that continued poor performance may lead to dismissal;
- a chance to explain: it may be that the tools are not right or there are other reasons why the employee cannot do that job:
- a chance to appeal: to prove that it is not just one manager who is antagonistic to the employee.

Redundancy. Unfair selection for redundancy occurs where an individual has been dismissed in a redundancy situation but is not the employee that 'should' have been dismissed. The tribunals identify the individual as having been unfairly selected if an agreed procedure or a customary arrangement has been breached. and there was no good reason for departing from that procedure or arrangement.

An employee who has been dismissed or is facing dismissal and who has 26 weeks' service can ask for a *written statement of the reasons for dismissal*. This must be supplied within fourteen days of the request being made. This provision is intended to help employees decide whether or not to make a claim for unfair dismissal.

Employees who are made redundant have three rights in addition to that of not being unfairly chosen for redundancy. These are the right to a redundancy payment, the right to consultation and the right to time off to look for other work.

Redundancy payments are made to all full-time employees with at least two years' service with the relevant organisation. Redundancies occur when a business closes down, or closes down part of its operation, or where some particular aspects of the work has ceased or diminished in total. It can occur, in other words, to anything from a whole company to a single individual.

The payments that must be made by the organisation must be at least the statutory minimum. They can, of course, be more by agreement. The statutory sums (part of which the company can claim back from a redundancy payment fund) are as follows:

- for each year of employment at age 41 or over but under 65 (60 for a woman): 1½ weeks' pay;
- for each year of employment at age 22 or over but under 41: 1 week's pay;
- for each year of employment at age 18 or over but under 22: ½ week's pay.

There is a maximum sum per week which changes regularly and a maximum number of years' service which may count: currently that stands at 20.

Consultation must take place about all redundancies. The company must notify the Department of Employment in such cases and, where a trade union is recognised, must consult with the union. For up to 100 redundancies the company must consult thirty days in advance, and if more than 100 redundancies are contemplated the company must consult with the union ninety days in advance.

Redundant employees who would be entitled to a redundancy payment must also be allowed *time off* to look for other work. In practice the company must pay for the employee's time off, up to a maximum of two days. It can agree to pay for more than two days if it wishes.

7 | Workplace industrial relations

So far we have considered what industrial relations are (in Chapter 1), looked at the main groups involved – management, unions and the state – and at the legal basis of industrial relations. But how does it all fit together? What are industrial relations like in British workplaces?

This chapter attempts to answer those questions. It will remind you of the range of workplaces and try to place industrial relations in their day-to-day context. We will examine the social structure of work and the potential for conflict, and outline some of the formal and informal methods and procedures by which such conflicts are handled.

The variety of workplaces

Self-check

Without looking back to Chapter 1 can you think of two or three factors which differentiate the kind of work that people do?

ANSWER

- The industry.
- Whether the employer is a public sector or private sector organisation.
- The size of the workplace.
- The occupations found there.

And there are many others. The variety of work is almost endless. Some people work in small offices, others in giant factories; some stay in one place, whilst others are constantly on the move; some jobs are clean, interesting, enjoyable; others are filthy and boring. There are many people at work who have a deep pride in the skill with which they perform tasks alloted to them; and there are many others for whom the task has been simplified so much that they feel they are merely a cheap robot.

These basic facts about work have an impact on industrial relations which may be obvious in some cases and less obvious, but still important, in others. Think about the places you have worked in, or know about, and try to keep them, and this huge variety of other workplaces, in mind as you read this chapter.

Industrial relations in context

In reading (or even in writing!) a book like this it is sometimes difficult to keep industrial relations in perspective. Although, as we have pointed out, industrial relations have a continuous bearing on nearly all work situations, we should not imagine that they are the subject of continual attention and concern in the workplace. It is easy, sometimes, to listen to the news on the radio and imagine that most people spend most of their time at work debating or even arguing about industrial relations. It just isn't so.

There will be occasions, in most workplaces, when industrial relations do come to the forefront: around the annual pay negotiations or in the event of a serious dispute, for example. But not only are such disputes rare in any workplace, but most workplaces never experience these moments of high tension. For most managers, and most employees, industrial relations are a vital part of the background to their work; only occasionally if at all do they push their way to the front of the picture.

There are individuals for whom industrial relations are much more than background. There are the industrial relations specialists in management that we considered in Chapter 2. For them industrial relations are a full-time job. Most organisations with more than a hundred or so employees have a specialist who deals with industrial relations. The title might vary (staff manager, office administration manager, personnel officer) and their jobs will be very different depending upon the style of the organisation. In some companies the specialist handles all meetings with the unions; in others they take a background role. This can become a contentious issue – we will return to it in Chapter 9.

Industrial relations may also be a full-time preoccupation with the union representatives we discussed in Chapter 3: the employee representatives and the full-time officials. Many of those who act as shop stewards or representatives whilst they are paid by their companies are full-time industrial relations specialists in all but name. Others devote varying amounts of time, from spending just a few hours a month on union business to spending just a few hours a month on their 'normal' work. For the full-time official employed by the union, of course, nearly all his time is devoted to industrial relations.

Activity

What about the manager who is not an industrial relations specialist? How much time does your boss, or a manager you know of, spend on industrial relations?

ANSWER

The question takes us back to the start of the book and our attempt to define industrial relations, and also to Chapter 2 where we argued that managers are people who get things done by or through other people. On the broader definitions at least, managers are involved in industrial relations nearly all the time – or, to be more exact, everything they are involved in has an industrial relations dimension. More than one manager has been known to complain that 'I could really get on with the job if I didn't have all these problems with the people under me', not realising that those problems are a central part of the job.

Even on a very narrow definition of industrial relations it is not sensible to assume for instance that managers who are not industrial relations specialists have little involvement with trade unions. There are more than a few people whose titles are factory manager or drawing office head or fleet manager, who spend most of their working day in discussions with union representatives or groups of workers. But they are exceptional.

Industrial relations surface as a separate issue only rarely, if at all, for most people at work. They are in reality an integral part of employment. From the employees' point of view, the jobs they have, the work they do and the way they are treated at work can all be seen as aspects of industrial relations. From the management's point of view, their job involves getting other people to do things, and that implies industrial relations.

In themselves these would be merely academic definitional points. They are more than that because within any organisation there is a wide variety of views and interests about what should be done and how.

Coordination and control

For any employing organisation to work effectively there must be some form of coordination between the individuals that constitute the organisation, and some form of control to ensure that the work gets completed according to a pattern. We saw in Chapter 2 that the interests and objectives of the individuals concerned will vary. Managers in general will have some interests in common with other employees and other interests that are at odds with those of other employees. Managers in different departments will have different interests.

It is a truism that everyone at work in any organisation has similar interests (such as in the success of the organisation). We have to recognise, however, that everyone will also have conflicting interests (such as who should be rewarded most if the organisation is successful). This is the paradox of work – and the reason for our concern with industrial relations. Every organisation requires coordination and control: but within every organisation there are conflicting interests. If it could be agreed that one group's interests should always override all others' there would be no problem. In a democratic society such agreement is not forthcoming; so we have to make arrangements by which these differences can be handled.

These arrangements have two broad aspects. There are, first, the *rules* which are laid down in the workplace, written or unwritten, to ensure the necessary coordination and control. Second, there are *procedures*, or steps that are taken to develop or enforce the rules. We will examine each in turn.

The rules

Self-check

Thinking back over what you have read so far, what kinds of rules might apply in the workplace?

ANSWER

You may have thought of all sorts of categories but most rules can be put under the following headings:

- Rules made by Parliament, which we have looked at in Chapters 5 and 6.
- Rules made by management; important in all workplaces and especially in workplaces where there is no, or only a very weak, trade union.
- Rules made by management and employee; remember the full scope of the contract of employment (p. 116).
- Rules made by management and union; these may, of course, be applied to non-union members too. We will look at how such collective agreements are made in a moment.
- Custom and practice; rules which in a sense have 'grown up' rather than been made. They are unwritten understandings about the way things are done in a workplace.

The objective of these rules is to ensure coordination and control in a way that reduces to a minimum conflict about the interests of those who are being controlled. The evidence of people leaving jobs, of apathetic workers, of absenteeism and lateness, of sabotage at work and of various forms of collective industrial dispute shows that industrial conflict exists nonetheless. However, as regrettable and sometimes disabling as such disaffection is, it is still occurring in only a very small proportion of possible cases. Most individuals at work accept the rules that apply to them.

How the rules are determined and enforced varies from workplace to workplace. One pivotal factor will be whether or not a trade union, or a number of trade unions, is involved in the process. Before considering the procedures in detail, therefore, it is useful to establish how a union becomes recognised by an employer as having a legitimate contribution to make in a workplace.

Trade union recognition

We saw in Chapter 5 that, legally, recognition of a trade union can come through an agreement between management and union, or be inferred from managerial actions. A series of legal rights follow once recognition has been granted. But what is recognition?

Self-check

Without looking back to Chapter 3 try to remember how the members are likely to judge their union. What do they join the union for?

ANSWER

There could be a lot of reasons, of course, but the main one is that they expect the union to achieve benefits for them in the negotiations that they carry out with the management. We will see in Chapter 8 that like the tango it takes two to negotiate. If management refuses to talk to the union representatives they cannot achieve anything. Once the management does start to talk to them it is said to 'recognise' them for negotiating purposes.

In practice, although there are a few exceptions, unions can begin to be of real benefit to their members only once they are recognised. Any degree of recognition entitles the union to the legal rights, but much more important in practice is the extent of recognition. There is a range – from only allowing union representatives in certain departments to accompany members during grievance or disciplinary cases at one end to a full involvement in all major decisions made by management at the other. Typically recognition is granted for something between these extremes. We should also note that neither the decision to recognise nor the extent of recognition is a once-and-for-all decision.

It is management that takes the decision to recognise a union.

In theory a union could claim that 100 per cent of employees were in membership and management could still refuse to recognise it. Unless management make a positive move to encourage the involvement of a union or unions in the workplace there is little a union can do to further its case. Obviously the members can strike in support of that recognition claim, and in recent years about one tenth of the strikes recorded have been in support of recognition claims. But strike action reinforces opinions about trade unions as harmful bodies whose sole intent is to disrupt work, and it will harm the establishment of the good relationship that the union is hoping to build up. So striking is a last resort.

Activity

If the decision to recognise or not recognise a union lies with management, why should managers ever agree to recognise trade unions? Try to think of at least two reasons.

ANSWER

It is not an easy decision. Managers will have weighed in the balance such issues as the time which they will have to spend dealing with union representatives, the imposition of a structure between themselves and individual workers and the powers which unions have to resist and modify managerial proposals. Eventually they will have agreed to recognise the union because of one or more of the following:

- pressure from unionised employees;
- pressure from outside (unionised workers in other companies that the management deals with, for example);
- a feeling that employees have a right to their own separate channel of communication;
- the advantages for management of dealing with a single group which represents many employees;
- the advantages for management of establishing a formal and accepted structure for handling conflict.

As we have noted, the decision to recognise can be changed or amended. There are a few examples of recognition having been

granted and then withdrawn. I was involved with a travel company that decided to recognise a union once the union had
established that one quarter of the staff had been signed up as
members. When the union official came back the following year
he was forced to admit that many of his members had left the
company (people join and leave travel agencies fairly readily)
and that the others were no longer paying their subscriptions.
The management withdrew recognition.

Withdrawing recognition once granted does not happen often
but the extent of recognition is more changeable. The most usual
changes are for recognition to spread from one department or
section of the organisation to another and often from one level of
employees up the scale to their immediate superiors, and on up
into management grades. The issues that are bargained over also
tend to widen, though this is a slow and patchy trend at best.
There is some evidence that when the economic circumstances of
the organisation decline collective bargaining focuses down on
job protection and pay.

The decisions on recognition and the extent of recognition are
key areas of management policy, and we will return to them
again in Chapter 8. At its widest, full recognition over an
extensive range of issues is often seen as a form of industrial
democracy, a subject we will discuss in more detail in Chapter 9.
The next aspect of workplace rules we will consider here is, in
one sense, the furthest development of trade union recognition:
the closed shop.

The closed shop

Recognition of a trade union to represent employees through
negotiation is one thing; an insistence that all employees should
join that union is another – and a much more controversial one.
This sort of arrangement is generally called the closed shop
although it is known in law as a union membership agreement. It
is arguably the most controversial issue in British industrial
relations.

There are in practice a wide variety of closed shop
arrangements, ranging from workplaces in which all employees
are union members and in which it is implicitly assumed that all

newcomers will join, to workplaces with very detailed written agreements between the union and management.

Like recognition, the signing of a closed shop agreement, and even the tacit acceptance of traditional 'all-union' arrangements, lies in management's hands. And in the manufacturing sector, to take one example, managements of about a third of all establishments with over fifty employees have granted closed shop arrangements.

Activity

Remembering (yet again) the value-laden nature of industrial relations, write down at least two arguments against the closed shop, and at least two in its favour. Closed shops were unlawful for a few years; do you think they should be allowed?

ANSWER

The case against the closed shop is usually made on one or more of three grounds:

- It is based on compulsion – employees who leave the union will be sacked – and that is fundamentally unfair and undemocratic.
- It can lead to injustice for individuals who do not agree with it and cannot therefore either get or keep a job in those workplaces.
- It gives the union too much power.

Deep-seated ideological beliefs often lie beneath these points against the closed shop. Whilst there are many people in industry who would accept these points, they are made most often by people who are not directly involved – politicians, newspaper leader writers and so on. The arguments in favour of the closed shop are more often made by the unions and management involved, usually on the grounds of the existing industrial relations position:

- It ensures that those who get the benefit of union work (all employees to whom wage increases, for example, apply) contribute to the unions; there are no 'freeloaders'.

- It ensures that the union is fully representative, of even the 'silent ones' who might not otherwise join.
- It prevents the incursion of other unions into established arrangements: there are no non-members for them to recruit.
- It ensures that disciplinary and grievance procedures (which we will consider in a moment) are equally applicable to all employees.

Your values will determine whether you think the closed shop should be allowed. It is widespread in British industry and in practice causes very few problems. There can be little doubt that most closed shops exist because the vast majority of employees want them, and managements find them useful. Legislative moves to protect people from possible injustice in the arrangement have not revealed great numbers of aggrieved individuals.

Procedures

Informal arrangements

Once the union, or unions, has been recognised for collective bargaining, and whether or not it has been granted a closed shop, managers and union representatives will have to establish a mechanism in which they can meet and negotiate. In practice there will, in most workplaces, be a range of mechanisms.

In many workplaces some, at least, of the arrangements are informal and *ad hoc*. Employee representatives will be free to talk to managers about any issue at almost any time and to resolve problems over cups of coffee or in a discussion in a corridor. This approach has great attractions for both parties and probably operates to some degree in most workplaces where the unions are recognised.

Activity

What are the problems of a totally *ad hoc* approach by management and unions to problem solving?

ANSWER

Solving the immediate problem is important, sometimes vital. The difficulties that can arise when informal, direct approaches are a favoured way to resolve problems tend to be longer term; they result in:

- differences in the way staff are treated in different departments;
- uncertainty about what the rules are;
- different interpretations of the same rule;
- lack of clarity about who is responsible for the maintenance of certain standards;
- concern on the part of those who believe they should be responsible, but who see problems solved 'over their heads', without their involvement.

In order to overcome these difficulties, and under the prompting of the legal requirements that we noted in Chapter 6, most organisations employing any substantial number of people have developed formal agreements.

Formal agreement procedures

There are two main categories of agreement. These are:

- *substantive agreements* – these concern the actual terms and conditions of employment, e.g. pay, hours and fringe benefits;
- *procedural agreements* – these are concerned with the rules of negotiation. You could liken them to the Queensberry rules for boxing.

Amongst these procedural rules are a number of different types. The main ones are:

- Disciplinary (including dismissal): initiated by management.
- Grievance: initiated by the individual.
- Disputes: usually initiated by a union representative.
- Consultation: initiated by management.
- Negotiating: usually initiated by the union.
- Redundancy: initiated by management.

Disciplinary procedures are concerned with the behaviour and performance of individual employees; grievance procedures are concerned with concerns that the individual has about the way he or she is being treated. Disputes procedures are the collective version of grievance procedures: when several employees have the same concern they invoke the disputes procedure. Consultation procedures are the means whereby management informs employees of a problem and takes their views into account before reaching a decision; negotiating procedures are usually initiated by the union, or unions, and decisions are reached jointly. Redundancy procedures come into play when management decides that it will reduce the number of individuals employed in a particular area or overall.

The procedures, which as noted above may be activated by different parties, take the form of a series of steps. If an issue is not resolved at one step it will be taken on to consideration by more senior people on each side at the next step.

For procedures to be effective they need to be credible. This means that employees need to see them as being reasonably fair and not as a device for delaying settlements for as long as possible. The advantages to management of good procedures can easily be underestimated. Amongst these advantages are that the various management representatives can feel more confident in knowing just what the decision-making procedure is and the precise part they play in it. Experienced negotiators can use procedures to define clearly what the problems are and, if they are not resolved, at least amicably agree what the points of difference are and who takes the next step. The emotional heat associated with disputes can lead to many misperceptions of the real issues, and good procedures skilfully used can do a lot to avoid unnecessary misunderstanding.

The development of joint procedures obviously can make dealing with employees and unions very much easier, but procedures do not exist in a vacuum. However good a procedure is it cannot compensate, for example, for inefficient working arrangements.

The range and form of procedures shows almost infinite variety. Some workplaces – civil service offices would be a good example – have very detailed negotiating arrangements, staff up to very high levels including many managers in union membership and a long tradition of dealing with all major problems at work through a process of consultation and negotiation. In some workplaces, issues such as pay and conditions are negotiated whilst other subjects, such as changing the work organisation, are left to management. This might happen in a retail store, for example. Engineering companies often have elaborate arrangements for the shop stewards and staff representatives to meet frequently to 'filter' the issues reaised by their members and to put the more serious ones 'into procedure'.

Workplaces vary not only in the arrangements they make for meeting to resolve conflicts of interest but also in who is involved. On the management side it might be certain levels of management at different steps, it may or may not include the personnel or industrial relations specialist; on the union side it might be the individual alone, the employee representative or the full-time official. Some organisations have what is known as an 'external' stage at the end of their procedures, whereby unresolved issues are sent outside the workplace for employers' associations and trade union confederation officials to resolve, or where a conciliator or arbitrator is appointed from outside both management and union.

Activity

What are the arrangements in your workplace, or in one you know of? Make a note of:

- the procedures that are written down;
- who is involved;
- if there is an external stage;
- how frequently they are used;
- the type of issues that are dealt with.

You may need to talk to a senior manager, an employee representative or a specialist to get a clear answer.

Why should there be such variety? What influences what is written and how it is used?

The individual procedures

The collective procedures are those in which management and unions are meeting to resolve disputes of interest that apply to numbers of, or all, workers. Such issues are comparatively rare, and the way they are handled is a key element of any organisation's industrial relations policy. We will examine them again in Chapter 9.

More common, and applicable to all employing organisations, are the individual procedures: grievance and discipline. The way they operate has a significant effect on industrial relations in the workplace, and we will now consider them in turn.

Handling grievances. When the relationship between the employee and the company is proving to be unsatisfactory to the employee then the employee is said to have a grievance. A grievance might be about an individual's pay or the kind of work they are asked to do; it might be about almost anything.

When an employee has such a grievance there are a lot of ways in which they can express it. If it is serious enough they might leave the organisation; this happens hundreds of thousands of times a year. But leaving a job is a hard choice, particularly if the employee is well paid, has a senior position or has been with the organisation a long time, and particularly with the present levels of unemployment. So many employees with a grievance will continue to work at their job.

The alternative to a thorough grievance procedure and a management style that encourages people to raise their grievances is that unhappy or discontented employees will complain to the wrong people, spread dissatisfaction, work without enthusiasm or perhaps act destructively.

It is to management's advantage if the grievance is expressed through a formal, accepted procedure so that it can be dealt with properly. This may mean correcting some information the employee has misinterpreted; it may be the opportunity to put something right that has gone wrong in the work or in relationships between individuals. Sometimes just airing the grievance, 'clearing the air', is enough. Even if the problem cannot be resolved it nearly always helps if the employee can see that it has been taken seriously and their concerns have been understood.

We have seen that the law requires managers to give employees a written statement which lets them know how they may take up a grievance. Procedures for the raising and handling of grievances have developed within the British tradition of voluntarism. They are agreements about the way issues will be dealt with, but they are not legally binding documents.

Table 10 (page 154), is a copy of a procedure in operation today. The main points to note are:

- The first step in nearly all grievance procedures is for the employees to raise the issue with their immediate boss.
- The levels of management and union involvement are clearly stated at each stage.
- The procedures stress resolution of issues as soon as possible. Some procedures put time limits on each stage to emphasise the point.
- This procedure has an external stage where 'third party' conciliation or arbitration is used when the two main parties (management and union) fail to agree.
- This company has an 'open door' policy so that any individual can talk to a senior manager at any time. Other companies would argue that this opens up the possibility of individuals 'bypassing' the procedure and would not allow it. What do you think?

Activity

Get hold of a grievance procedure, preferably from your own place of work. It will be different from the one in table 10. Consider how it is different, why that may be and the practical implications of those differences from anyone with a grievance working in either company.

A final point to make about grievance handling is that a rough-and-ready '90 per cent rule' seems to apply in almost every workplace. This is that 90 per cent (more or less) of grievances are satisfactorily resolved at the initial discussion with the supervisor. Of those that go into the formal procedure, 90 per cent (more or less) are resolved at the first stage; of those that are not,

90 per cent are satisfactorily concluded at the second stage, and so on.

Table 10. Example of an individual grievance procedure

The right of any employee, whether a member of a trade union or not, to request a personal interview with his department head shall be in no way limited by this procedure. It is accepted by all parties to this agreement that the most satisfactory solution to a problem results when agreement is reached between the individual and his superiors. The procedure for handling requests or complaints is for use in the event of the parties being unable to agree. Every attempt will be made to deal with grievances as soon as possible. If the union representatives feel that there has been unnecessary delay the industrial relations manager and the union official will investigate the complaint. The stages in the procedure will be:

Stage 1
The employee having a request or complaint arising from his employment will raise the matter with his appropriate superior and together with him every effort will be made to resolve the problem. Failing settlement the employee will proceed to the next stage in the procedure.

Stage 2
The employee and his local representative, if requested, will meet the employee's respective manager. Failing settlement the matter will be referred to the appropriate senior managers or their deputies. A report of the proceedings will then be submitted to the industrial relations manager and where applicable to the full-time official of the union.

Stage 3
Without undue delay, a meeting will be arranged between the individual concerned, the trade union's full-time official, the local representative, the industrial relations manager and the appropriate management representative.

Stage 4
Failing settlement at stage 3, the matter may be referred by either party to the Advisory, Counciliation and Arbitration Service for conciliation;
   or by mutual agreement the company and the trade union be taken to independent arbitration through the Advisory, Conciliation and Arbitration Service. In this event the decision of the arbitrator(s) will be final and binding on both parties.

Handling disciplinary cases Grievances occur when the relationship between the employee and the organisation is proving to be unsatisfactory to the employee. When the relationship is proving to be unsatisfactory to the management there may be a case for disciplinary action.

Just as grievances may be resolved more or less constructively in all sorts of ways, with procedures as only one possibility, so may disputes about the employee's behaviour or performance. The employee may be dismissed and a replacement hired on – usually a time-consuming and expensive process. The poor behaviour or inadequate performance may be tolerated, with much private moaning by the managers concerned. This happens all too frequently. Sometimes the employees (and the problems) are transferred to another department.

There are more positive approaches: carefully designed training, a new challenge or the use of appropriate disciplinary procedures.

Activity

What is 'discipline'? Write out for yourself some alternative words that you might use as part of a definition.

ANSWER

The dictionary definitions have the following elements. 'Discipline' (as a noun):

- instruction;
- branch of learning, or field of study;
- training;
- mode of life in accordance with rules;
- subjection to control;
- order;
- severe training;
- mortification;
- punishment;
- an instrument of penance or punishment.

'To discipline' (as a verb):

- to subject to discipline;

- to train;
- to educate;
- to bring under control;
- to chastise.

It is interesting how far down the list is the idea of discipline as punishment. However, this is still a common view of discipline in many work organiations. Managers are often told – sometimes by me! – that discipline should be seen as a corrective and preventive measure, putting the employee back on the right path, rather than as a punishment for going wrong. The corrective approach is both more humanitarian and more cost-effective, but we have no way of knowing how many managers use discipline this way in practice. In theory it is clear that the aim of disciplinary action is to ensure that the breach of standards is not repeated either by the individual (or group) being disciplined nor hopefully by others.

There is a lot of guidance available to anyone involved in disciplinary procedures. You may remember from Chapter 5 that there is a code of practice on disciplinary practices and procedures and from Chapter 6 that the industrial tribunals are requiring managers to take certain steps before a dismissal will be judged fair. By inference many of those steps are taken as part of a disciplinary procedure.

Table 11 outlines some of the main advice given in disciplinary procedures in the code of practice. Table 12 gives some practical advice on the way disciplinary cases should be handled.

Activity

Consider the disciplinary procedures in your organisation or one you know of, against the advice in the code of practice shown in table 11. Does that procedure meet the standards laid down? If not, in what ways does it fall short?

Consider too the *practice* of discipline. In the organisation you are considering is it generally seen as corrective or punitive? Do people get away with too much, or is management harsh? Are most cases handled fairly? (You may need to talk to other people in the organisation to decide the answers to these questions.)

Table 11. Code of practice advice on disciplinary procedures

Disciplinary procedures should:

(a) Be in writing.
(b) Specify to whom they apply.
(c) Provide for matters to be dealt with quickly.
(d) Indicate the disciplinary actions which may be taken.
(e) Specify the levels of management which have the authority to take the various forms of disciplinary action, ensuring that immediate superiors do not normally have the power to dismiss without reference to senior management.
(f) Provide for individuals to be informed of the complaints against them and to be given an opportunity to state their case before decisions are reached.
(g) Give individuals the right to be accompanied by a trade union representative or by a fellow employee of their choice.
(h) Ensure that, except for gross misconduct, no employees are dismissed for a first breach of discipline.
(i) Ensure that disciplinary action is not taken until the case has been carefully investigated.
(j) Provide a right of appeal and specify the procedure to be followed.

Table 12. Advice on handling disciplinary cases

- Gather together the facts including precise details of the standards that should have been reached; ensure that there really is a problem and decide what standard the employee should be achieving.
- Consider whether there was a written rule, and whether the rule has been enforced. Did the employee know about the rule?
- Give the employee a chance to give his side of the story, in private. Encourage a two-way conversation; consider the employee's replies and, if necessary, adjourn the meeting while you consider any new facts.
- Check on the company's own procedure to see what the next appropriate stage is if you are not satisfied with the employee's replies: should you be giving an informal, formal, oral or written warning?
- Whatever disciplinary action is taken ensure first that it is appropriate and that 'the punishment fits the crime'. Ensure that the employee understands why you are taking the action.
- Consider what effect action will have on other employees.
- Ensure that written warnings detail, in specific terms wherever possible, what improvements are expected, within what period of time, and the consequences if the improvement is not made, is insufficient or is not maintained.
- Monitor the employee's behaviour following the disciplinary action.

Non-union methods

In addition to the arrangements agreed with or involving the trade unions, there are methods of resolving disputes of interest at work which do not include the unions. Some of these methods are found in organisations which recognise trade unions as well as those which do not; others are found only in non-union firms.

In the first category – methods which do not include the union but are found in unionised as well as non-union firms – we can include:

- a range of management controls;
- a series of information-passing and consultative arrangements;
- informal relationships.

Management controls operate in every organisation and even in the most participative only a few of them are the subject of collective bargaining. It is most unusual, for example, for the unions to influence a department's budget or financial targets for the year. However, these may be very important in industrial relations; they can make some solutions to problems possible, others almost impossible. Other conflicts of interest may be obscured or resolved through a performance appraisal system or a work reorganisation or through retraining. Only in a minority of cases are the unions involved in such decisions. We will examine these areas of managerial prerogative in Chapter 9, on management policies.

Consultative arrangements and methods of passing information up and down the organisation are rarely limited to a union-only channel. Consultative meetings, such as safety committees, shop councils, social committees and progress review groups, all perform a valuable function in helping individuals and managers to cope with differing interests as well as in achieving their ostensible aims. And there is now a vast amount of money being spent each year on purchasing the advice of consultants who will advise on 'briefing groups', 'quality circles' or whatever the latest fashion in passing information may be. These are all channels to which the union has no formal access.

Informal relationships are in many ways the most important means of resolving different interests. It is in the nature of management that much of a manager's task includes the informal coaxing, cajoling, 'jollying along' of subordinates that is almost indistinguishable from social conversation. The most effective line managers are often those who are most skilled at developing and using these informal methods. This is an aspect of management that is far from the high-powered jet-set, executive image that is sometimes portrayed. But this unglamorous part of the job is perhaps the part where most *potential* conflicts of interest between managers and employees are handled and prevented from becoming serious disputes.

Activity

Could all potential conflicts of interest be handled through the three methods outlined above? If your answer is 'no', why not?

ANSWER

The answer is 'no'. Even the most informal, non-union organisation will have some procedures laid down by which employees can progress grievances and be disciplined. These are, after all, legal requirements. And of course where a union does exist it will be trying to ensure that it has an input to mechanisms laid down for resolving conflicts of interest. Nor should we assume that, because an organisation does not recognise a union, its arrangements will all be informal.

We could make a distinction between ununionised and non-union organisations. We could call *un*unionised those companies which have not recognised a trade union, which hope, probably, that they never have to, but which have got no long-term and detailed policy to keep the unions out. The *non*-union companies we could identify as those which have developed a consistent and detailed policy designed to ensure that they never have to recognise a union. They may have set up their own 'staff association' to which they grant many of the facilities that elsewhere a union might enjoy. They will often have a complex and well-established system of communication and consultation with groups of staff, and policies aimed at keeping staff grievances to a minimum and handling them through a procedure that is seen to be fair when they arise.

Decisions about the degree of formality and whether or not to involve a trade union in handling conflicts of interest are key features of a company's industrial relations policy and will be considered in Chapter 9.

Summary

We have seen then that the freedom which British employment law grants to the parties in industrial relations and the wide variety of managements and trade unions have led to tremendous diversity of practice at the workplace. No two workplaces are alike. No two workplaces have the same industrial relations.

In very few workplaces are industrial relations a central preoccupation. Rather, the conflicting interests of management and employees are handled in a variety of ways, only some of which are normally understood to come under the heading of industrial relations. In most workplaces other than very small ones trade unions are recognised and there are established negotiating arrangements. In addition to the collective procedures developed specifically to regulate the relationship between managers and unions, the trade unions are also heavily involved in individual grievances and disciplinary procedures. Even in the most highly unionised companies, however, the informal arrangements still play an important part in workplace industrial relations.

Activity

Consider the formal and informal arrangements in your workplace. Or think of one you know about, or have read about. If there was a scale of formality, ranging from 10 – most formalised – to 0 – totally informal – how would you rate your workplace? And, thinking of the problems that have arisen, or could arise, do you think it should be more or less formal?

8 | Negotiating

In this chapter we look at the practice of industrial relations negotiating. You will, if only through reading the newspapers, know something about this already. This chapter could, if you work through it carefully, make you a better negotiator. This is important because, although there are many subjects which management claims to be non-negotiable, there is an increasing number of topics which *are* being negotiated. Ten years ago management generally did not expect unions to be interested in a new sales campaign or pensions provisions. At present they are involved with pensions but not with the sales campaign. In ten years time, who knows?

What is 'negotiating'?

Consider these snippets of conversation.

Alan: I hear you have a push-bike for sale Beryl?
Beryl: That's right.
Alan: How much do you want for it?
Beryl: £50.00.
Alan: OK, I'll take it.

Colin: That radio set in the window – has it got long wave as well as medium wave?
Dawn: Yes, sir – FM too.
Colin: It seems quite reasonably priced.
Dawn: It is, sir. It's the last one in the shop and it's been in the window so it's a bit faded. We've knocked 20 per cent off the price.
Colin: Would you knock another 5 per cent off?
Dawn: I'm afraid I can't, sir. That's the shop manager's job. But I don't think he would go any lower.
Colin Hmmm.
Dawn: It is a good deal, you know, and they've been selling fast.
Colin: OK then – you've talked me into it! I'll take it.

Errol: So, if it's that good, why are you getting rid of it?
Frank: We just don't need a car safety seat now that the boy's growing up.
Errol: You've had it a long time, then. £10 is quite expensive.
frank;   Not compared to new. And we've only had it a year.
Errol: I didn't want to pay more than a fiver.
Frank: Well, I might go down a bit: but not really below £8.
Errol: Suppose I offered you £6.
Frank: You've only increased your offer by £1. If I dropped to £7.50 you'd have to collect it.
Errol: OK, OK. £7.50. I'll call round on Sunday and take it, then.

Activity

Are these negotiations? Look up the definition of 'negotiation' in a dictionary.

ANSWER

It will vary slightly according to your dictionary. The *Oxford English Dictionary* defines 'negotiation' as 'to confer with another with a view to compromise or agreement'.

Self-check

So, how many of those conversations involved a negotiation? Just on first impressions choose one, two or all three.

ANSWER

Well, the first was a straight sale. In the second, Colin tried to get into a negotiation about a further reduction in price, but Dawn forestalled him. Only the third was a real negotiation.

What then do we mean by a negotiation? We can see that it is closely related to things like selling, trading and even, perhaps, arguing.

Activity

What distinguishes the third conversation from the others so that we can say that it is concerned with negotiation? Take three minutes to write down two or three factors.

ANSWERS

Of course, there are many distinguishing features. But for the purposes of defining this conversation as a negotiation we should note particularly:

- the two parties involved have different interests;
- they communicate about these differences; and, crucially
- they are both prepared to move towards each other from their first stated position.

You may well have noticed other differences as well and we will look at some of these later in this chapter.

With this definition we can distinguish 'negotiation' from similar words like

'consultation' – where there may be no view to compromise;
'problem-solving' – where there is no conflict of interest;
and 'selling', 'diplomacy', or 'trading' – which may or may not involve compromise.

Activity

How many places in which people negotiate can you list in three minutes?

ANSWER

The complete list would be endless, ranging from the United Nations to the corner shop. Other obvious ones would include a Middle Eastern bazaar, a car showroom, a trade union office, the Stock Exchange or your own doorstep.

If your list goes beyond this, and you are sure that these are cases where two parties with different interests are talking with a view to compromise, well done!

Industrial relations negotiations

A lot of negotiations, of course, takes place in industrial and commercial organisations, and a lot of that is industrial relations negotiation – about the terms and conditions of employment and the way work is organised.

One thing that our definition indicates is that negotiation is not limited to the formal set-pieces over the annual pay deal that come to most of our minds when we use the word. Undoubtedly the bulk of negotiating in British workplaces is done standing by a machine, or at someone's desk or in a corridor. It is often these informal, apparently casual negotiations that keep the wheels of business turning. The best managers and employee representatives are well aware that they *are* negotiating in such cases.

Negotiation is not a private activity. In the first place it involves at least two sides. Each side will be trying to impress and persuade the other. If there is more than one person on each side, as is often the case in industrial relations, then the members of each team will also be aware of their colleagues' reactions. Behind each side there are other groups: the board of directors and the union membership may not be in the room but they are not forgotten. Neither are other companies in the industry, or the union hierarchy, and in many negotiations the public (via the press) are also interested.

This can be represented diagrammatically – see figure 3.

Negotiation is a *spectator sport*! (Or, at least, it has features in common with spectator sports.)

Conventions

In spectator sports the players are often 'acting' for the audience, may be influenced by the audience and will be expected to follow certain unstated rules or approaches. In a football match, for example, we expect players to celebrate when they score a goal, and we expect the goalkeeper to stay inside his penalty area during the game. No formal rule says they must, but if they do not it is a matter for comment.

We can call these expected behaviours 'conventions'. There are two problems in identifying them. The first is that they tend to become accepted as the 'way of life' or what is 'normal'; we do not notice the goalkeeper staying in his area unless he moves out of it. The second problem is that conventions vary from place to place; in ice hockey it is quite acceptable for the goalminder (or a substitute) to leave the goal unminded in some situations.

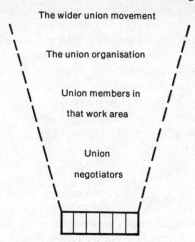

The wider union movement

The union organisation

Union members in
that work area

Union
negotiators

Industry, the Government, the Press

The General Public

Management
negotiators

Senior managers
in the companies

Board of Directors

Shareholders and other
companies

Figure 3.

Activity

Chose a negotiating situation that you know about; either from experience or from the newspapers. Can you identify any of the conventions here? Do not take more than three minutes to think about it.

ANSWER

You may find it hard to come up with many conventions because as we noted above, they are conventional – accepted and not easy to notice. In many organisations in the UK (and elsewhere perhaps) some or all of the following negotiating conventions would be expected to apply:

- Management and unions sit on opposite sides of the table.
- First demands are always more than either side expects to get.
- Neither side will withdraw offers once made.
- Both sides change their stance only to move towards each other.
- Both sides allow adjournments.
- Management do not personalise conflict.
- Things can be said 'off the record'.
- Key decisions are recorded in writing.

Conventions will vary from industry to industry and between organisations. (So you may have identified several that we have missed.)

What is important about conventions lies in what happens when they are *not* followed. Take the one that 'offers made are not withdrawn'. A few years ago the National Union of Seamen were negotiating with their employers, and at one point the employers told the press that as the seamen would not accept an offer it would be withdrawn. Almost immediately there was an outcry from some newspapers and from the seamen, who accused the employers of 'cheating'. The employers quickly made a new and more acceptable offer.

By breaking the convention, the employers risked being seen as untrustworthy. They certainly raised the temperature of the negotiation. In general, unless it is as a carefully calculated tactic, it is important that we are not seen as 'odd' or 'strange'. We need to know the relevant conventions and to follow them.

> *Self-check*
>
> Which conventions were *not* followed in the discussion between Alan and Beryl about the bike on p. 161?

ANSWER

The answer would be almost all of them, as they never got into a negotiation. In particular we might note that:

- the whole thing was complete very quickly (speed is dangerous in negotiations);
- the first demand was accepted;
- neither side tried to gather any more information about the subject at issue (was it a good bike? A big one? What sort of bike?).

The more important and formalised negotiations are, the more likely are the participants to stick rigidly to the appropriate conventions. It is the safe thing to do. The conventions ar ignored at the negotiator's peril. Only in very rare, almost 'life or death' situations, might experienced negotiators defy the conventions in an attempt to bring home to the other side how desperate the position is.

> *Activity*
>
> Consider a situation that you know from work or from the newspapers. List five of the conventions that you would take care to follow if you were negotiating there.

The power position

Power is important in negotiations, because if one side has great power and the other has very little this will obviously affect the outcome of the negotiations. In industrial relations each side needs the other: the employer needs to have staff as much as they need a job. Neither side, therefore, is ever completely powerless. Even where one side has a dominant position at any point, it is aware that it will have to work with the other side in the future. This is why experienced negotiators tend not to go for all-out victories; they try always to 'leave the other fellow with at least his bus-fare home'.

We should be especially aware of two aspects of power. Firstly, it changes. Neither side is ever completely powerless, and the relative positions will move over time and depending upon the issue. In a retail operation, for example, the employees may well have more power towards Christmas when the shops are expecting to do a lot of business; they may have much less in the summer when many of them are most interested in their holidays. On the other hand, an airline may be most vulnerable during the summer, when more passengers will use it. We have all read of the Easter holiday strikes in air transport.

The issue at stake will be important too. It may not matter to bank employees who takes first turn on the counter, and consequently the employer has the power to change that around according to his interests. It may not be so easy for him when it comes to changing their hours of work. On this issue they may well feel strongly and the employer will find himself in the middle of a negotiation.

The second aspect of power is that it can only be felt or guessed at and not measured exactly. If both you and I *believe* I am powerful, then I am. If my side has a very real power to stop the business, but I am not aware of it (like many computer programmers, say) then my power in negotiation is very small.

Activity

How could an employer who knows he has to negotiate with the trade union over pay in six months' time try to build up his power position? Take two or three minutes to note down three approaches.

ANSWER

The key point to realise is that either side can influence its power position. You may have thought of many way; just as examples we could mention:

- telling the union representatives well in advance that the company is not making much money;
- asking managers and supervisors to check employees' feelings about the pay rise they expect to get;
- announcing a pay freeze on all top salaries;
- getting managers of strategically placed workers to let them know that they will get more than the others;
- declaring that no new staff will be taken on for six months whilst the company talks to the unions about ways of avoiding redundancies.

None of these, or any of the other strategies you may have thought of, is risk-free.

The bargaining range

Whatever the power position there will be an area over which the negotiations will take place. In our example where Errol was buying a child's safety seat from Frank the range was from Frank's £10 to Errol's £5. We can see the same pattern in an industrial relations negotiation.

Activity

The union has claimed an increase in pay of £8. Management has said it is not prepared to offer more than £2. The union hopes to get around £5 and will not settle for less than £3.50. Management would like to settle for £3 and will not go above £4.50.

Can you represent these positions by means of a diagram with two parallel overlapping lines? What is the 'bargaining range' of these negotiations? What is the likely 'settlement area'?

ANSWER

Your diagram should look something like this:

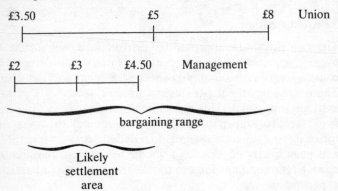

We can call the sides' opening position their *demand* (D), their realistic preferred position their *target* (T), and the point beyond which they will not go their *resistance point* (RP).

Activity

Include these positions (by their initials) on your diagram for each side.

ANSWER

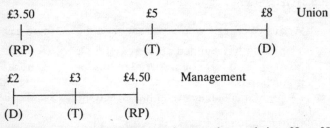

The bargaining range is between the two demands i.e. £2 to £8, the whole area within which the negotiations may move. The likely settlement area will be between the two targets, unless (as here) one side's target is beyond the other side's resistance point. This will be a tough negotiation.

Let us take each of these points (demands, targets and resistance) in turn.

The demand

The two sides' opening positions, or demand, will define the overall bargaining range (if we are in a society which accepts the convention of moving only towards each other and not apart). There is some research evidence which shows that the more extreme your demand the more likely you are to get a settlement favourable to your side. This is because you pull the bargaining range in your direction, change the other party's expectations and have plenty of room to manoeuvre. But this research has mostly been conducted in buyer-seller negotiations in classroom experiments.

In real-life industrial relations there are many examples to show that demands that are too extreme can be dangerous. Not long ago the British Steel Corporation, which was losing a lot of money, offered its workers a 2 per cent pay increase when the average in other industries was about 12 per cent. There was an immediate strike. The BSC management had to raise its offer substantially to get negotiations started at all. This led to a severe loss of credibility and BSC ended up giving a pay increase at least on a par with the average.

Self-check

What two criteria would you say should determine a negotiator's demand?

ANSWER

The key criteria, which pull in opposite directions, are:

- room to manoeuvre ('make it high');
- credibility ('keep it reasonable').

The target

In most negotiations, the target will be more complicated than in our simple example. It is likely that even in this case (see p. 169),

the union might have wanted an increase in pay of £5; or perhaps
£4 with a few extra days' holiday. similarly the management
might have been hoping to keep the wage bill down, but may also
have wanted to negotiate the introduction of a new way of
working which would be more efficient.

Targets often include more than one element. The skills of
negotiating include:

- Being very clear about you own targets. Discuss them before
  you get into negotiations. Make sure they are realistic, that
  they can be achieved. Would a different 'package' of results be
  acceptable?
- Assessing the other side's targets.

When targets are more complex than these, assessments become
very difficult. The more complicated, multiple targets change the
situation. Instead of our diagram looking like this:

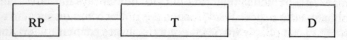

We now have to see the situation as:

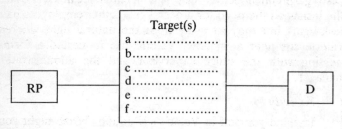

A, b, c, d, e and f will be alternative targets that we will aim for.
For example, if we were the managment negotiating overtime
pay, 'a' might be an increase in pay with an overall decrease in
the amount of overtime; 'b' might mean a smaller increase in
overtime pay, no decrease in the amount of overtime but
increased flexibility in where overtime can be required; and so
on. The other side may well have an equally complex list of
targets.

Nowadays some companies have developed sophisticated computer programmes that 'cost' various packages, so that, in adjournments, they can assess the relative values of various proposals. Most negotiators, however, still manage this by assessing a list of target packages (such as 'a' to 'f') before the negotiations and using these as benchmarks. Alternative packages can then be estimated by reference to them ('it's not as good for us as "d" but its probably better than "e" ').

In most negotiations each side will have some things that it is prepared to concede from its opening demand. Each side will probably also have things that it is *not* prepared to concede: the resistance points. Between the two there are a number of objectives that they would like to achieve and some will be more important than others. The question is: which are the most important ones for you, and which for the other side?

Remember too that even apparently straightforward cases may not be so simple. People do not always declare their objectives in negotiations; indeed it is not uncommon for at least some of the people involved not to be aware of their underlying objectives.

Consider Valerie's desk-light.

Casting light on objectives Valerie is an employee in a city office. She insists on the need for a desk-light. Other employees have desk-lights but they sit away from the natural light whereas Valerie sits near a window. Valerie has requested a formal meeting with the office supervisor and the administration manager.

Activity

Imagine yourself in Valerie's situation. What might your objectives be?

If Valerie brings in an employee representative to the meeting what might the representative's objectives be?

Imagine yourself as the office supervisor. What are your objectives now?

If the administration manager does get involved what might his objectives be?

(List one or two possible objectives for each person involved.)

ANSWER

You may have a vast range of objectives depending on how imaginative you are. Some of the more straightforward ones include:

for Valerie
- getting a desk-light;
- receiving equal recognition with other employees;
- calling attention to some other aspect of her situation;

for the representative
- helping Valerie to achieve her objective;
- establishing a precedent that could be used elsewhere;
- showing that a representative could help employees;
- establishing a rapport with management;

for the supervisor
- not committing his company to spending money;
- not establishing precedents;
- remotivating Valerie;
- keeping the office manager at a distance;
- involving the office manager;

for the manager
- speedy resolution of problems;
- supporting the supervisor;
- establishing a rapport with the representative.

Resistance points

Negotiators may find themselves at a point where they would rather the negotiations broke down altogether, with all that that might mean in terms of industrial action or unhappy workforces, rather than concede. I have called 'resistance points' those commitments or objectives which the negotiators are not prepared to give up at all.

The resistance point may be an issue of real principle, such as a union's demand for recognition as a bargaining agent (see Chapter 7), or it may be a point on a scale, such as a sum of money which one side or the other will not accept.

Negotiators are often less clear about their resistance points than they should be. Some experienced negotiators still confuse this with their target. In such cases it is not surprising that they often end up having conceded far more than they should have done.

Activity

How should a negotiation team decide upon its resistance point? Take three minutes to write down two or three guidelines.

ANSWER

Resistance points, like demands and targets, should be established by discussion amongst the team, before the negotiations begin. They would take into account factors like:

- What can we not give up at any price?
- What financial state is our organisation in? How will the issue we are negotiating affect that?
- What would be the result of the negotiations breaking down on our side?
- What would be the result on the other side?
- How far would we be backed if we broke off negotiations at this point?

Activity

Consider a negotiation that is happening at the moment. Look at the story in three or four different newspapers. Can you, from the newspaper reports, assess each side's opening demand, target and resistance point?

ANSWER

From the limited information available from the press can you identify the bargaining range and the likely settlement area? (If the answer is 'yes' make a note of it; if the answer is 'no' – what would *your* demand, target and resistance point be in each party's position?) Remember to check back when this is resolved to see how close you were.

Preparing for negotiations

So far, then, we have established that negotiation is a complex activity in which two people, or two teams, try to resolve differences of interest by a process which leads to compromise and agreement. We have noted the existence of conventions and the impact of power. And we have considered the bargaining range and the importance of being clear about demands, targets and resistance points.

We should now be in a good position to start examining the actual process of negotiations. Normally, we would start by preparing ourselves prior to the event. Sometimes that may not be possible; we may get stopped in a corridor, or a subject that we thought did not need negotiating may suddenly become a negotiating issue. These situations are dangerous – if possible, we should delay until we have had a chance to prepare.

In most cases we will have some time for preparation.

Activity

Write down three general headings under which we might start our preparation. Think of the ground we have covered so far in this chapter, but do not take more than a minute or two.

ANSWER

Our headings will vary, depending upon our view of which topics can be put together under a heading, but you should have included the following:

- assessing the bargaining range;
- getting together our facts and arguments;
- working out our tactics and preparing our team to carry them out.

It might be useful to spend a short time on each element.

Assessing the bargaining range

This would include making sure that we were clear about our

objectives and that we have discussed the possible objectives that the other side may have.

We should also ensure that we are clear about our own demand and resistance point and that we have established, as closely as we can, the various packages that might make up an acceptable or a desirable target. This may involve discussions outside the negotiating team. The team itself, or you yourself if you are negotiating alone, should also have attempted to identify the other side's likely demand, targets and resistance points.

Facts and arguments

This is what most people think about when they consider preparation for negotiations. The amassing of facts is relatively straightforward and most people are quite good at it. It may involve some detailed research into, for example, settlements elsewhere, or the financial state of an organisation.

Nothing is more embarrassing for a negotiator than to find that the other side knows something he does not, or that the material he has got together is in some way wrong or inaccurate. But if facts were all that were important then negotiators (and perhaps even managers as an occupational group) could be replaced by computers!

What prevents the computer taking over is that there are issues of power and skill involved too. If the facts are against you but the power is on your side you are in the position of a robber holding a gun on a rich man; you will still get the result you want. Or if the facts are against you but you are a skilled negotiator you may still get what you want; like the cunning fox who outwits a whole pack of hounds.

In industrial relations, facts are rarely neutral. Take the following five statements about the cost of living:

(a) Inflation increased 10 per cent last year on the government's figures.
(b) It is predicted that the cost of living will go up 15 per cent in the next twelve months.
(c) The cost of living increase will make the workforce 15 per cent worse off next year.

(d) The wages paid by this company buy 10 per cent less now than they did a year ago.

(e) This year the company has been able to charge higher prices and so make more money because of inflation.

All are accurate reflections of the facts at a point in time, but the implications of each statement are different.

Self-check

Which of the five statements would be most useful in persuading a group of employees to put in a high wage claim? Which would be most useful in putting that claim to management?

ANSWER

Statement (c) is most likely to persuade the employees, and (e) to be most useful in putting the claim to management. The reason is that these two statements present the facts in a way that is most likely to make these two groups of listeners aware of the implications for them personally. Not that they will necessarily be persuaded by those arguments, but they are at least likely to be aware that the speaker understands the relevance of those facts to them.

So gathering the facts is only half of this part of the preparation. Those facts then have to be considered in terms of 'arguments', points that can be argued with the other side. That means casting the facts in a light that will show the other side how those facts are meaningful to them. In turn that may mean that some of the facts that have been collected will be discarded – because although they are undeniable facts, they cannot be made directly relevant to the opposition.

Skilled negotiators generally use very carefully selected arguments to back up their points. They have found that, by advancing only a few arguments, they can ensure that their points are strong and relevant. If they advance too many the other side will wait until they hear one that is weaker, and then attack that one. These skilled negotiators gather their facts, make them relevant to their opponents and then select only those few that will be really strong for use in the negotiations.

All this may seem a little cynical, but this is the way it happens. Other approaches (like total honesty) may be morally preferable, but have been found to be extremely risky. And most negotiators are too aware of their responsibilities to take risks.

Tactics and teamwork

The third aspect of preparation that we identified was planning the tactics, and the teamwork to carry out those tactics. As with any situation involving human beings it is not sensible to plan too rigidly. A negotiator must be prepared to adapt his tactics to cope with events.

Nevertheless, most negotiators will go into each set of negotiations with a framework of tactics that they will follow. The best negotiators have the ability to adopt different tactics in different situations. They will decide whether to start 'reasonably' or 'aggressively'; whether to hold out a long time before the first concession or to try to get to that stage early; whether to try to gain their key points first or leave them till later; whether to try to squeeze some small 'extras' at the end, or not. And they will be conscious that their opponents will be doing just the same.

The negotiators will also want to sort out the roles, or 'parts', almost in a stage or film acting sense, that the members of their team will play.

Activity

What roles could members of a negotiating team fill? Take three minutes to write down at least three possible roles that team members could perform.

ANSWER

There are many possible roles and you may have thought of some quite unusual ones. The most common fall into two types. First, those connected with some task:

- chairman;
- secretary/note taker;
- financial expert;
- numbers man;
- spokesman.

Then there are those connected with certain tactics:

- aggressor/attacker;
- peacemaker;
- scapegoat.

If there is more than one on your side it makes sense to increase your options by having the team perform different roles. A cricket team with specialist batsmen, bowlers and wicket keeper is always likely to beat a team composed entirely of bowlers. Furthermore, you are even more likely to be successful if your team knows what roles each member is supposed to fulfil, and if you have discussed how you might use the various options.

If you have not had a lot of experience of negotiating you may have to work quite hard at these roles. You will choose them by reference to the skills and aptitudes of your team members, by what they feel happy doing, and in relation to the issues to be negotiated. There will be no point in having a 'numbers' man if you are not discussing anything involving numbers. Experienced negotiators will be able to do this much more quickly:

> Well, Jim, I'll act as the spokesman and you and Joan can chip in as appropriate once we've got the opening demands out of the way. Will you keep notes of what they say and check out how they react, visibly, to our claim? Joan, I'll pull you in on the details of the working methods. Let yourself go on the angry, aggrieved and disappointed bit, especially the first time I call you in. OK?

And in they go to face the other side.

It isn't easy to fake emotions convincingly unless you are a star actor so it's just as well to limit yourself to the task roles. If you have got the personalities for it, though, many negotiators like the 'rubber cosh and cigarette man' tactics. The police have found that many individuals submit to interrogation when faced first with an aggressive, heavy, threatening interrogator who is entirely negative and then by a friendly, helpful one who offers cigarettes and a sympathetic ear. It sometimes works in negotiations too.

The point about roles is that there are options. You should plan your team's tactics in this respect so that all the members know what they are expected to do and how they fit in. It is not unusual for disagreements within the negotiating team to be at least as fierce as those with the other side. The key requirement here is that the debates within your team are not reflected in the negotiating room. There you want to look as united as possible.

The stages of negotiation

Often it is difficult when we are involved in the hurly-burly of a negotiation, even a simple one involving two people, to appreciate what is happening. We will get better results if we are aware of the various stages through which negotiations tend to go, and can see which stage we are in as we progress.

We can start by using a simple analysis. All negotiations will have:

- a beginning;
- a middle;
- an end.

Words like 'tense', 'angry', 'formal', 'fun', 'casual', 'aggressive' and 'relaxed' have been used to describe negotiations. Some will be more typical of each of the different stages.

> *Activity*
>
> Write down the words 'beginning', 'middle' and 'end'. Against each, write down, using some of these words or your own, what you might feel like at each stage of a negotiation.
>
> Also against each word ('beginning', 'middle', 'end') write a few words to describe what might actually be happening: arguing, giving a summary, taking notes, making introductions, etc. Use your own words.

ANSWER

'Beginnings'
You may have written down words like:

formal	introductions
tense	opening demands
expectant	rejection
long-winded	supporting statements
polite	

The first stage of negotiation is usually formal. The participants will be introduced to each other with their job titles or negotiating role ('chairman of our side'). Experienced negotiators will go through these formalities in order to establish themselves and their position even when they know the other side well. The rest of the beginning will vary with the situation but will usually be polite, collar-and-tie style. If it is a major negotiation with two 'teams' they will sit on opposite sides of the table whilst their chairman makes a (usually fairly long) presentation of their case – and the other side rejects it.

In less formal negotiations the presentations of the case may be less cohesive and involve a good deal of question and answer. Even in these cases, however, the early phase of the discussions will include at least one side making its demand and having it rejected, more or less explicitly, by the other.

In formal negotiations at least, the 'end of the beginning' is often signalled by an adjournment when both sides leave each other to reflect on what they have discovered.

Activity

Apart from making your own demand in the beginning you must also receive theirs. Making sure that you fully understand their position without making any commitment can be difficult. List three tips for someone receiving someone else's demand.

There are a great many possible tips. You might have included some of the following:

- Challenge each point they make.
- Make sure you understand each point fully, even if that involves repetition.
- Try to assess the strength of the other side's commitment to each point.
- Do not betray emotion, unless well calculated.
- Ensure that you have the complete demand, with all points understood, before committing yourself on any.

'Middles'

You may have written down words like:

aggressive	arguing
untidy	challenging
emotional	disputing
strained	emphasising difference

but you should also have words such as:

constructive	concessions
relaxed	compromise
togetherness	trade-offs
hard-working	narrowing of differences

In fact there are two phases to the middle of a negotiation. The first stage we might call the 'testing' stage. Here both sides try to emphasise to each other that the demands are deeply felt, that their claims are just and well founded and that they are not prepared to move very far from them. At the same time they try to establish which points the other side feels most strongly about, which points they might concede and how far they are prepared to go with their case.

This phase often involves challenging of facts and disputing of arguments, is sometimes loud and aggressive, occasionally personal and always tense. Collars and ties have been loosened, the room may be filled with smoke, and coffee cups may be spread around. The neat piles of paper that could be seen in the beginning stage have now been spread all over the table – and perhaps beyond. Everyone will have become involved in the discussion.

The second part of the middle we can call the 'moving' stage. At some time in the course of the negotiations the two sides have got to start moving towards each other. This can be tricky, particularly when they have both spent a lot of time telling each other that they are not prepared to move . . .

We will look in a moment at how we can switch from one stage to another. Once this switch has been made, however, and concessions have been made, movement towards each other starts and it can build up a momentum of its own. We are all familiar with the term 'horse-trading' – it is used to signify the situation typified by two gypsies. They spend some time looking over the horse, the buyer pointing out loudly a lot of imperfections whilst the seller praises all the animal's good points. Eventually they feel they know as much as they can about the horse; and the negotiating then can be fast and furious:

– £100.

     – £50.

– £80.

     – No more than £60.

– Say £75 then.

     – £70?

– Done!

The momentum is typical of the moving stage of negotiations – though perhaps as negotiators in industry we should try to end our 'horse-trading' without the gypsies' habit of spitting on hands and slapping them together!

Activity

Obviously one of the important points in the 'moving' stage is the making of concessions. A concession is a move away from a position that you have said you cannot move from! So it has to be handled carefully. Take three minutes to list two or three points to bear in mind when making concessions.

ANSWER

You might have noted that:

- Concessions are, eventually, expected in all negotiations.
- Small concessions are best: they keep credibility, and you may get a larger one in return.
- You should give concessions only in response to pressure.
- Concessions should only be made in return for concessions – do not give unless you get.
- Concessions made too early in a negotiation only show the other side that your first demand was too high.
- Concessions should be made carefully – plan them or discuss them with your team in an adjournment first.

It's no tea party . . .

Some people do not enjoy negotiating. It's so impolite, they will tell you, and to an extent they are right. Not that anyone should be rude in negotiations, of course, but the rules in negotiations are different from the rules in everyday society. In everyday conversation we would try:

- not to be repetitive;
- to build up the other people involved;
- to be succinct;
- not to be aggressive; and
- not to say things we do not mean.

In negotiations, however, we must be prepared:

- to repeat ourselves continuously (stamina is crucial);
- to undermine our opponents;
- to be patient and take our time;
- to be aggressive; and
- to be convincing about points we are ultimately to concede.

It is not rudeness. It is just another example of understanding the rituals and rules of this unusual game. Perhaps it's because the social rules do not apply that other people enjoy negotiations so much!

'Endings'
Words you might have written down to cover endings might include:

formality	agreement
respect	repetition
carefulness	summaries
congratulations	statements about future

Or, of course, the negotiations may have ended in failure, in which case many of these words would not be appropriate. The end of a successful negotiation is where the two sides have reached a mutual position that both can at least accept, even if they may not like it.

Self-check

The problem with endings is that you have at each stage been trying to convince the other side that your position is final. Can you think of anything that will convince the other side that you really have reached your final position?

ANSWER

There is no simple answer. The following may help you to convince them:

- You make it increasingly difficult for the other side to win concessions.
- There is a clear difference between this offer and the form of previous concessions.
- You suggest making the offers public in some way.

One experienced negotiator used to emphasise the fact that he had reached his final position by gathering up his papers and shutting his briefcase. What that led to, unfortunately for him, was that everyone got to know he still had concessions to make until he packed up his briefcase!

Usually the differences between the two sides will narrow increasingly as each makes concessions, until there is very little between them. The end is in sight. By some means, often a summary of the negotiations so far, the two sides will settle on a final outcome. At this stage, for industrial relations negotiations at least, three things are beneficial:

- Summaries: so that both sides know what they are agreeing to.
- Clarity: a form of words both understand. Writing it down will be useful for the future.
- Follow-up action: the negotiators must go back to their sponsors (the audience of our spectator sport), tell them what has been agreed and try to ensure that it is put into effect.

Activity

You have finally reached an agreement on a difficult issue. What do you do now? (Write down two or three things that should be done immediately after the negotiations are complete.)

ANSWER

Well you'll probably want to relax and celebrate. But there are a few tasks to be completed first. These will include:

- committing the agreement to writing and having it approved by the other side;
- notifying the key individuals on your side of the results;
- making sure that any action you have agreed to is put in hand.
- where necessary arranging a follow-up meeting to check on the way the agreement is working;
- arranging for members of your side to meet to assess what you've learned from the event.

Now you can celebrate . . .

Activity

Consider a dispute that is currently in the newspapers or on television, or one that you know about at your place of work or in the locality. What stage is the dispute at? What are the next moves likely to be?

The negotiating process, then, goes through four stages: beginning, testing, moving, ending. In practice these stages may not follow each other quite as neatly as this for one of two reasons. First, the process may repeat. We may get all the way through almost to agreement on issue number one and then have to go back through testing and moving on issue number two before we can reach an overall agreement. Second, we may get it wrong.

Activity

What would be the effect on our negotiations if we tried to move on to the next stage before the other side was ready to do so? Think of each stage and then write one sentence to summarise your conclusion.

ANSWER

Well, we will all write different sentences but they will all indicate something negative. That is why it is important to understand the stages that negotiations go through. If I try to get on to testing before I've got all the details of your demand you may surprise me unpleasantly later. If I try to start moving whilst you are still testing you will take that as evidence that I did not really hold the views I stated, absorb my concession and so narrow the bargaining range in your favour. And if I try to end the negotiations too soon you will be able to squeeze extra concessions out of me – and in life many negotiators find themselves giving too much away right at the end.

Tactics in negotiations

When people first see a skilled and experienced negotiator in action, particularly if he is facing them, they often wonder how they can hope to compare. Gradually, though, as they gain experience themselves, they see that there are a number of tactics that these negotiators use which can be learned and copied.

We cannot cover the full range of tactics here, but four of them warrant particular mention. These are:

- Questions.
- Summaries
- The hypothetical statement.
- Adjournments.

Questions

Skilled negotiators use a lot of questions. They find that questions have three major uses. First, and most obvious, is that they elicit information. Information about the strengths and weaknesses of the opponent's position; about the elements that have been included in his case, and more importantly, those that have been ignored; where he stands firm and where he might be prepared to move; whether the understanding of a given problem or issue is common to both sides or whether there is a difference; and precisely where and what the agreement is as it builds up during the negotiation. Without such probing it is difficult to identify where and how to proceed to settlement. Questioning is therefore an essential part of negotiation.

Second, questions control a conversation. If I make a statement you may support or oppose it, or ignore it entirely. But you are very unlikely to ignore my question altogether; you will respond to it in some way. The question therefore controls what you will talk about next.

Third, the question shows that you are taking notice of the other side's case. In the beginning and testing stages this may indicate that the questioner is listening carefully, cannot be bamboozled and is unlikely to fall for a sloppy or sneaky argument. In the later stages it may show interest in the other side's point of view and problems.

Some questions are better than others.

> *Activity*
>
> Take two minutes to write down three tips on how to question effectively.

ANSWER

You should have included some of the following points among your three:

- Ask one question at a time (your opponent can only answer one at a time; you can ask the others that may be in your mind later).
- Repeat the question, or ask a related one, if not satisfied with the answer.
- Try to avoid questions which can be answered by 'yes' or 'no' unless you are trying to show the opponent that he agrees or disagrees with you. Questions using 'what' 'how' or 'why' are usually best.
- Short, sharp, clear questions are best.
- Once you have asked the question, stop. Do not be afraid of silence to try to fill it in with your idea of what the answer should be. Silence puts pressure on the responder.

Summaries

Experienced negotiators also use more summaries than novices tend to use. They summarise their own arguments regularly; they summarise the key points, as they see them, of their opponent's case – and leave the opponent to correct their summary if they wish. This ensures that both sides are clear about where they stand.

The skilled negotiator also summarises the course of the discussions at frequent intervals. This brings home to those involved how much, or how little, progress has been made. It helps to give the negotiations a sense of structure.

Summaries can also be useful in cooling the atmosphere when it becomes heated; and in changing the mood generally.

The hypothetical statement

A vital skill in negotiations is that of suggesting movement or concession whilst not making any commitment. This is often done by means of the hypothetical statement, 'If I did x that might change the situation'; or the hypothetical question, 'If I were to move to x would that make it possible for you to forgo y?'

> ### Self-check
>
> Why is the hypothetical statement or question so valuable in the moving stage of negotiation?

ANSWER

If you remember our discussion on concessions (p. 184) this should be quite straightforward: the hypothetical statement is a way of checking that the other party is prepared to move before making any commitment. The link with a concession from the other side is made before the offer of concessions is made concrete.

Adjournments

In negotiations it is quite usual to have breaks, or 'adjournments' as they are known, in which one or both sides withdraw and reconsider their position. These breaks may last just a few minutes with one side stepping into the corridor to check a single move such as a new offer. They may last an hour or so, with both sides in separate rooms reviewing what they have discovered about each other and replanning their tactics. Or they may last weeks, with each side contacting their members or seniors – or just getting on with other business.

Adjournments can just be breaks taken as necessary, though it has been argued that an iron bladder is the real key to successful negotiations! Often, however, adjournments are used tactically.

Activity

When might an adjournment or break in the negotiations be valuable? List as many situations as you can in three minutes.

ANSWER

Adjournments have many uses. They can be taken to:

- provide a breathing space when people are tired;
- allow reassessment of targets and progress;
- plan new moves;
- allow us to report back to our side;
- provide the opportunity to end one stage of the negotiations and move into another;
- avoid committing ourselves;
- enable us to move without loss of face;
- emphasise that we cannot move any further.

Example of a summary

Activity

In order to summarise this chapter let us assume that a friend of yours (who has not read it) is about to get involved in an industrial relations negotiation for the first time. This friend has asked you for a sheet of paper to take into the negotiations: 'Give me three tips on what to do before the negotiations start; three tips on what to do during the negotiations; three tips on what to do at the end and three on what to do afterwards.'

If this chapter has met its objectives (see p. 161) this

should be a good opportunity for you to consolidate your learning. By now you will know what negotiating is, how you can analyse and affect power, how to identify the key elements of the bargaining range and how to prepare and conduct negotiations. Take five minutes to write out a dozen tips.

The tips you have included will vary according to your assumptions about the kind of negotiations in which your friend is getting involved. This chapter has included dozens so you will have had to be selective: they might include the following:

Before the negotiations start

- Try to create a positive climate.
- Gather your information.
- Assess each side's strengths and weaknesses.
- Try to estimate the other side's targets and resistance points.
- Decide on your own objectives and opening demands.
- Establish your targets and resistance points (and write them down).
- Consider possible tactics in the negotiations.
- Choose your negotiating team.
- Allocate roles.
- Make sure everyone is clear what you are trying to achieve, and how.

During the negotiations

- Listen carefully to the other side.
- Take your time.
- Keep your cool.
- Use a lot of questions.
- Make use of summaries.
- Try to be clear about what stage of the negotiations you have reached.
- Make good use of adjournments.
- Develop your teamwork.
- Try to stay fresh and alert.
- Make your concessions in small steps, and get something in return.

At the end of the negotiations

- Be cautious about offers that are announced as 'final'.
- Always leave the other team with something to claim as a victory.
- Summarise.
- Put the agreed terms in writing.
- Congratulate your team and theirs.

After the negotiations

- Ensure that everyone on your side who was not negotiating knows what was agreed.
- Ensure that the agreement is implemented.
- Monitor the results of the agreement.
- Prepare the climate for the next negotiation.
- Review the negotiations with your team.

In negotiations, as in all other areas of management and industrial relations, experience as such does not mean much. The only way to improve your negotiating skills is to negotiate. However, that will lead to an improvement only if you take the trouble to learn from your negotiations. To do that you need to be aware of the process and prepared to take the time to sit down with your negotiating team after each negotiation and examine the way it unfolded. 'Do it and review it.' Good luck!

9 | Management policies

It has been a theme through this book that, of the three main parties to industrial relations – management, unions and the state – it is management which has the major responsibility for developing and maintaining industrial relations at the workplace. At this point we should look at managerial policies in industrial relations, to see what it is that managements are, or could be, trying to achieve and how they are, or how they could be, planning to meet those objectives.

Trends – the small scale

In societies such as Britain where economic growth is no longer virtually automatic (and that includes most societies now), a key problem can be summed up in the word 'performance'. If we *can* do something and we *want* to do it, then we can achieve a level of performance. We can see it as an equation:

performance=can×want.

At national, company and individual level what we *can* do is expanding enormously. We now have sophisticated machinery, robotics and computers that enable small groups of individuals to produce the goods or provide the services that it took thousands of people to produce or provide only a few years ago. Even where the jobs have not changed all that much in terms of technology our ability to organise the work more rationally and our more sophisticated training techniques have had an impact on what we can do.

Increasingly, however, the problem is becoming what people *want* to do. People are no longer so prepared to work hard for ten or twelve hours a day, six days a week, fifty or fifty-one weeks a year. And if they did they would still have a whole series of other requirements that would influence the way they work and what they could be expected to do.

People now have rising expectations about the conditions they will work in, how clean they are, how safe, how socially enjoyable. They have expectations about the way they will be treated in terms of material reward, but also in terms of status and respect. And they have ideas about how *they* would like to see the work organised, the product or service sold, and the results invested.

Managing industrial relations

One approach to these issues argues that, as technology develops, it replaces jobs that people were doing in industry, commerce and the public services. Therefore, it is said, industrial relations become less important. An alternative approach is that industrial relations *are* becoming less important because economic difficulties place management in the ascendancy, so they need not worry about how they manage employees. We have mentioned the counter-arguments: that increased technology in a post-industrial society puts more power in the hands of the man or woman who controls the computer; and that in troubled economies it is more important to manage employees properly so that their hopes and concerns are met and they want to perform effectively.

Activity

Take a few minutes to think around some workplaces you know. What effect is new technology having on them? What is your view of the future of man management at the workplace?

Whatever your views about the future of man management, it is clear that, in the next few years at least, industrial relations will continue to be important because:

● For the state, efficiently managed staff, a lack of industrial disruption and a constructive relationship with the trade unions will be central to economic improvement.

- For the employees and their unions, employment, and the way people are treated at work, will be vital to their well-being.
- And for management, good industrial relations, and the policies to bring them about, will be prerequisites for success.

Industrial relations policies

We can define an industrial relations policy as 'a set of proposals and actions that act as a reference point for managers in their dealings with employees'. This is wider than some other definitions which assume that a policy has to be written down. Our definition implies that all organisations will have some form of policy because, in all organisations, managers and other employees will be able to establish what the senior executives will tolerate or encourage in the treatment of staff. In some companies, the 'cowboy' building or road haulage firms for example, the policy amounts to no more than a general understanding that they will do whatever they can get away with provided it brings in the cash.

Most organisations have more complex policies – although in only a minority of cases as yet will the kind of attention and planning proposed in the rest of this chapter have led to the development of the policy. In most organisations the industrial relations policy has developed in a fragmented and piecemeal way.

'Espoused' policy and 'operational' policy

We can distinguish two forms of policy. One is the more narrowly defined industrial relations policy formalised in managerial statements and documents which outline sets of principles or procedures. In the jargon this is called the 'espoused' policy. It explains what management would like to achieve in its industrial relations if possible.

Managers are sometimes guided in their actions by the espoused policies. Their problem is, however, that the subject of industrial relations for the line manager is only rarely identifiable as a separate topic. In most cases it is bound up with the day-to-day running of the workplace. The way staff are treated is much more closely related to the way work is organised and carried out than it is to the espoused policy. The managers organise the work according to the pressures and priorities placed on them by senior management. These pressures come in the form of demands for some type of output from the manager's section – products or services. These pressures and the priorities that they indicate lead the manager to act in certain ways and avoid acting in others. Because these pressures and priorities are also controlled by senior management it is sensible to talk of these too as a policy: the 'operational' policy.

In practice the managers try to follow the operational policy: to do what it is that senior managers want them to do, taking account of all the priorities and problems. Managers down the line will follow the espoused industrial relations policy only where it is part of the operational policy.

In general this chapter will be talking not about the broad statements of principle which managements sometimes issue, but rather about the operational policy. We will be less concerned with whether management has issued a document stating that it will consult with shop stewards, for example, than with whether arrangements are made and managers checked to ensure that such consultations take place. Our concern is with the practical way that senior executives indicate by word and deed that some things are required from line managers, whilst others would merely be good provided that they did not interfere with more important matters like production or sales or customer service. It is after all this operational policy that determines the way managers behave, to a large extent at least, and hence has a significant impact on industrial relations.

In some few organisations planning of these operational policies is changing. One or two of the larger organisations in both the public and the private sector are beginning to look critically at the way senior managements influence the treatment of employees. They are seeing that manpower and industrial relations can be planned, controlled and managed in the same way as any other resource – except that it is more important and perhaps more complex.

Industrial relations objectives

Activity

Write down three or four words which might summarise what management is aiming for in its industrial relations policies.

ANSWER

You might have written down any of a large number of words depending upon the type of management you were thinking of. Most of them will fall under the following general headings:

- simplicity;
- control;
- stability and predictability;
- efficiency.

You might have included in your list an objective of industrial peace or the absence of conflict. That will certainly remain a key objective for most managements. But it is less central to modern policies because managers are coming to see that the policy of peace-at-any-price is shortsighted. The other objectives outlined are more important and sometimes worth the risk of disruption. Furthermore, continuing high levels of unemployment, amongst other things, means that the number of strikes is reducing anyway. Peace will continue to be a desired aim, but as a contributor to other objectives rather than a separate one.

You might also have included in your list some idea of fairness or justice, and some requirement to abide by the law. These are principles that all managements will need to state in any written policy and they will be criteria that most managers will try to follow. In the operational policy, however, these will be methods to achieve the sort of objectives we have indicated above.

Let us now consider each of the four general policy objectives in turn.

Simplicity

One of the first objectives to which managers will turn their minds is simplicity. First because the complexities, and the associated problems, of industrial relations are all too evident in many companies. Managements are faced with a multiplicity of unions often antagonistic to each other, and a multiplicity of bargaining arrangements, leading to a highly varied and complex wage structure. Managements will aim to simplify all these arrangements.

The simplest arrangement is where management negotiates one annual wage increase with one union which covers all members of staff. Such a system is, practically speaking, unobtainable in many workplaces in Britain. It has been handled in the past by developing joint union arrangements within the workplace, or by creating a variety of different bargaining units. These approaches will continue, but there are alternatives which a management that wants to lead rather than respond can adopt.

Managements will be aiming to reduce the number of bargaining units to as few as possible. Bargaining units – the different groups with which managements negotiate – can be simplified by amalgamation so that fewer negotiations take place, or by reducing the number of unions within each group. The first option is to some extent under managerial control; they are one of the parties to the negotiations. The second option is not; but managers can have some influence on the strength of particular unions.

Managers can influence the success of particular unions. They can develop strategies of allowing one union in an area to achieve 'victories' handling grievance or disciplinary cases; they can be seen to be treating one union with more respect, involving it more than another. These are long-term strategies, but they can be successful in limiting the appeal of the trade unions in one area to a particular union that managers are trying to encourage. Greater simplicity will have a number of benefits for managements, including:

- the saving of managerial time (one or two sets of negotiations rather than seven or eight);
- the removal of barriers between groups (hence making it easier for employees to accept moves from one group to another).

Activity

Think about your own workplace. How complex are industrial relations there? How could they be simplified?

Control

A central aim of many managerial policies in industrial relations is control of manpower. This will be achieved, in some cases, paradoxically by moving away from the idea of control through employment, but in most instances will involve an extension of control in the workplace.

Control outside employment is already commonplace in some areas. Certain services are traditionally performed by employees of other organisations, or by self-employed people. Window-cleaning and accountancy, secretarial 'temps' and security services are typical examples. This tendency may spread. There have been recent newspaper reports of local authorities 'contracting out' various tasks, such as refuse collection, that have traditionally been performed by council employees – and many private companies are doing the same thing. Control of the *contract* is by price and service; control of *staff* is delegated, as it were, to the contractor.

Within the workplace control operates very differently. We have discussed disciplinary rules and procedures. More and more supervisors are being trained to operate such procedures effectively. Indeed supervisory and management training of all kinds is expanding.

Disciplinary procedures are only one form of control that management can adopt. Some controls are built in to budgetary systems or to machinery. If a production line moves at a particular speed, that will itself control how fast the employees there work; management has to do little to control at least the speed of their work. Similarly new computerised programmes allow managers to see very easily how much work their subordinates are doing, and how effective that work is. Other controls are to be found in performance targets, in monthly and quarterly reports on the work of the department or in annual performance appraisals.

Of course all controls by management may be opposed by the

trade unions and their members. In the present situation, with high levels of unemployment, the unions' power may be muted. Some managements are using the opportunity to establish or re-establish their control over employees in an aggressive way. The more sophisticated ones are establishing which controls are most appropriate for them and ensuring that they operate in a way not seen as threatening by the trade unions.

Activity

List six ways in which management in your workplace tries to ensure that employees are performing their work appropriately. For each of them consider: is this form of control accepted by the employees? Is it effective? Will it be used in the future and, if so, will it be changed or modified in any way?

Stability and predictability

A third objective managers will be trying to achieve in industrial relations is stability. The fewer unplanned occurrences the better. Management will therefore be attempting to establish and maintain systems and procedures that handle conflict effectively and without disruption of the work.

The communications systems within management can usually be improved. Managers are trying to ensure that clear messages and information are passed down the hierarchy to non-managerial employees. They are attempting to be as receptive as possible to the concerns and grievances of their staff. Supervisors assess morale and try to deal with small issues before they become major problems.

The policy will aim to ensure that issues which are more important or cannot be easily resolved are directed through established channels. Detailed grievance procedures will be developed, with the trade unions where appropriate, so that employees have a formalised and accepted method of resolving issues that may develop into conflict. For issues that involve groups the organisation may have a separate 'disputes procedure'.

Stability should not be confused with absence of conflict or lack of change. The first is unobtainable in an industrialised society; the problem is not the existence of conflict but whether it can be handled effectively and used constructively. A lack of change should worry any management. Organisations which remain the same in our rapidly changing environment will soon be outmoded. Change will occur. If the industrial relations arrangements within the organisation are effective they will be able to facilitate change without compounding the difficulties by being continually in flux themselves.

The impact of more extensive information passing, both up and down the organisation, and of more detailed and elaborate grievance and disputes procedures, will be to give managements more warning of areas of conflict. Other proposals include a more formal link between negotiation groups, within and outside the organisation, so that the danger of 'leapfrogging' – each group alternately jumping above the other in wage or salary terms – is reduced.

These factors will contribute towards the linked objective of 'predictability'. One obvious way of increasing predictability would be to extend the period of agreements. At the end of the 1970s and in the early 1980s it was already becoming common, especially in the public sector, for wage and salary agreements to last for fifteen or eighteen months. The declining rate of inflation during this period was an important factor: when employees were confident that the value of money would not decrease too much over a longer period they were prepared to accept longer-term agreements. In future, managements may start looking for pay deals that last two or even three years. These are common in some countries already; they may become more usual in the UK.

Activity

How stable and predictable are industrial relations in your workplace? What, if anything, are the specialists doing to make them more predictable? If you are not sure – go and ask them . . .

Increasing predictability in industrial relations will enable managers to start planning ahead, directing and coordinating the human resources within the organisation in much the same way that they can do with resources such as cash or machinery. Like those resources, they will be aiming to use manpower as efficiently as possible.

Efficiency

Perhaps the main thrust of industrial relations policies in many organisations in the future will be towards efficiency.

There are definitional problems when we use a term like 'efficiency' in relation to manpower. The efficiency of an engine or a computer can be agreed and measured; we can measure for certain factors in manpower, but not for others. And there is often disagreement about the criteria we should adopt. Let us take an example. Warehousemen empty and stack lorries as they arrive at the warehouse. Suppose, through scheduling or traffic difficulties, no lorries arrive during the afternoon, then several arrive together, necessitating overtime by the warehousemen. Has their efficiency gone down? (Manpower costs to unload the same number of lorries have increased.) Should the men be asked to do something else whilst waiting for the lorry? What could they do that would leave them free to start unloading as soon as a lorry arrived?

Efficiency, in a manpower context, has two components: keeping costs as low as possible, and increasing output. Keeping costs down traditionally involves employing no more people than necessary to do the job and employing them as cheaply as possible. It is now understood that this is too narrow a view of costs. Keeping the numbers as low as possible, for instance, may mean that big new contracts have to be passed up, because the organisation is not geared to cope with them. And employing staff as cheaply as possible may mean that the organisation has poor quality staff, with little training, no enthusiasm to do the job properly and little commitment to their present management.

The more sophisticated managements are, therefore, taking a fresh look at their manpower costs. They are trying to establish, through manpower planning systems, what numbers and what kind of manpower they will need, and what they will have to offer in order to attract such manpower. Keeping costs to a minimum will remain an aim but will be subordinated to the other objectives. This involves a sharper, more hard-headed look at manpower costs than traditional 'hire 'em when it's good; fire 'em when it's bad' approaches and may lead to a different wage and benefit package or structure, and sometimes to higher pay for the individuals working in those organisations.

On the cost side, then, the trend is for a reduction in costs, but set in the context of rigorous examination of the manpower requirement of a particular organisation. On the output side managements are trying to:

- increase labour flexibility;
- increase commitment; and
- extend the range of bargaining.

Labour flexibility

> *Activity*
>
> What are the factors that reduce management's ability to use any employee in any appropriate task? Think about a workplace you know, or work in, and try to identify some of these restrictions in labour flexibility.

ANSWER

You may have identified all sorts of things, depending on which workplace you know. But you will probably have noted four main types of restriction:

- restrictions imposed by law;
- restrictions arising from a lack of capability to do particular tasks;
- restrictions arising from managerially determined divisions within the workforce ('division of labour');
- restrictions arising from employee determined divisions within the workforce ('demarcation').

These categories overlap somewhat so you may have a little difficulty in fitting your answer in. The categories help us, though, to understand the types of restriction that there are on labour flexibility and how an industrial relations policy might aim to cope with it. This is important because it has been argued that it is the inefficient way that manpower is used in the UK which has to some extent caused Britain's economic problems. If people are unable or unwilling to move from one task to another as required then some tasks will not be done, or will be done only after a delay, or will need more people to be employed than is necessary to get the work done.

Legal restrictions on flexibility are, as we have seen, very limited. There is some restriction on the working patterns of women, young persons, pilots, drivers and so on but the law in general stays out of this area of employment.

Lack of capability is perhaps the major limitation on management's use of labour. If individuals simply cannot do a task then they cannot be used for it. Managements are developing a series of policies to resolve this problem. They are organising new training and retraining initiatives. It was frequent in the past for people to stick to the same specialism throughout their working lives. In future people may have half a dozen or more different types of job. So employing organisations are arranging training programmes to cope with this.

An individual employee is also restricted in what they can achieve, in their efficiency, by the technology at their disposal. The pace of technological change is advancing rapidly, something we will discuss in detail in Chapter 10.

Division of labour, the splitting of tasks between individuals, is one of the main features of a developed economy. It is arguable that we could not have the wealth we enjoy today if we had all continued to try to provide everything for our own needs. The idea of the division of labour is central to all ideas of scientific management. Many of the divisions within the workforce, and the development of barriers which it is difficult to cross, have been instigated by management.

Breaking down some, at least, of these barriers is now a focus of many industrial relations policies. The reason is that the pace of change is now so fast that what seemed to be sensible divisions not very long ago are now inhibiting progress. They do not look so sensible. Divisions between manual and non-manual workers become a problem when manual workers have to programme computer-aided machinery, or when managers want clerical employees to do overtime for which they have not traditionally been paid. Many companies are now adopting policies of 'harmonisation' – establishing identical conditions of employment (other than salary, and some service-related privileges) for all employees. This has the dual benefit of (1) being seen to be fair and (2) promoting flexibility: there is no financial reason why an employee should not switch from one task to another.

Demarcation problems arise when the employees decide that a particular individual or group, and only that individual or group, should perform a particular task. Everyone has heard stories of the workman whose machinery goes wrong, but who cannot fix it until a trained electrician has come along to unplug it! (Because electrical things like plugs are electrician's work, whilst mechanical work on the machinery belongs to the engineer.) Thus two men, and a long delay, do work that could readily be done by one – but for demarcation.

It has been a feature of the industrial relations policies of many organisations to negotiate out such demarcation lines. This is difficult whilst other divisions continue. Today's division of labour is often tomorrow's demarcation dispute. Increasingly private sector organisations are moving towards the 'single status' position of the civil service or some Japanese companies, where the boundaries are reduced to a minimum so that employees are prepared and enthusiastic about moving from one task to another as required.

Activity

We have so far examined the advantages to management of having a flexible workforce. Can you think of any advantages to the non-managerial employees?

ANSWER

You might have thought of quite a few, depending on your experience and your imagination. Commonly quoted advantages are:

- it is fairer if everyone's treatment is the same;
- it makes work more interesting if you can do something different now and again;
- it may mean that your company can compete better, and your job is more secure;
- it enables employees to develop their abilities and skills.

Increasing commitment There are already very few workplaces where a manager could rely on 'dumb obedience' to get the work completed. It has often been pointed out that the best way to sabotage almost any organisation would be to obey orders to the letter: no more and no less. In practice all organisations rely on a measure of interest, enthusiasm and creativity on the part of their employees. As technology advances jobs are likely to become more complex, or even more boring – or both! Managers will need to develop industrial relations policies that make people want to work; they will have to generate motivation and commitment.

Activity

What steps could be taken in your organisation or one you know of to generate motivation and commitment? This is an important question; try to write down at least three specific proposals.

ANSWER

Almost everything has been tried and some steps work sometimes. It will depend on the workplace you are thinking of. Amongst other steps managers might consider:

- increased participation in decision-making;
- increased information about the organisation and its performance;
- sabbaticals: time off to study or 'recharge the batteries' in some other way;
- fairer disciplinary handling;
- salary-linked or other incentives for good performance.

Extending the bargaining range Traditionally it has been the unions who have argued for an extension in the range of bargaining, and management which has fought to restrict it. This may be changing. The unions are increasingly concerned to concentrate on job security and wages. It is now managers who are putting new factors into that debate: getting trade unions to negotiate on quality control, on disciplinary standards or on the distribution of incentives.

Extending the issues which are negotiated in this way has the benefit to management of bringing the 'output' side of the contract of employment into focus and avoiding a complete focus on the 'costs' side. It also commits the union representatives involved in the negotiation (morally at least) to ensure that the quality is maintained, or discipline improved or whatever other change is agreed. Bargaining about employees' output is still uncommon, but it may become more widespread.

Developing the policies

These objectives – simplicity, control, stability, predictability and efficiency – will be included amongst the aims of most managerial industrial relations policies in the future. Each organisation will also have other objectives, and the policies that organisations develop to achieve their objectives will vary enormously. It is now better understood that the policies adopted by an organisation must be closely related to its particular situation; only very general principles can be borrowed from other groups or from the guidance contained in codes of practice.

This means that whilst the objectives that we have considered so far in this chapter are likely to be held to some extent by all organisations, no two will apply them alike. For a small company in an expanding and competitive market the needs of efficiency may well be paramount and the management prepared to forgo the other objectives to some extent. For a large bureaucracy the objectives of simplicity and control may carry most weight. Not only will the balance of these objectives vary, but the way each objective is translated into an operational policy will be different in each organisation. A management consultancy might rely heavily on a policy which linked pay clearly to income generated; such a policy would be simple, relatively under control and stable, and apparently does much to motivate the consultants. Such an approach would not be feasible in a social services department.

Exactly how policies are developed will also vary. In many companies and public sector bodies industrial relations policies are at present assumed to be the preserve of the industrial relations specialist.

Activity

Can you foresee any problems in giving the responsibility for industrial relations policies to the appropriate specialists? Try to identify at least two points.

ANSWER

The problems are implicit in our discussions of management's role in industrial relations in Chapter 2 and in parts of this chapter. In brief they might include the following:

- The specialist may be somewhat divorced from the day-to-day managment of staff; so the policy may be inappropriate as a guideline for managers.
- The specialist may not have access to the top decision-makers; so the policy may remain an espoused policy rather than be operational.
- The specialist may have different understandings of policies that the organisation has in other areas; so may develop industrial relations policies that conflict with, say, financial or customer-service policies.
- The specialist may not have the authority to enforce aspects of the policy on line managers; so the policy will lose credibility.

You may have thought of others.

These kinds of problem have contributed to the lack of effectiveness that industrial relations policies are sometimes accused of having. Companies have responded in several ways. An increasing number have elevated the industrial relations specialists to the board of directors, thus putting them in amongst the power holders and increasing their authority. Other companies have moved in the opposite direction, reducing their personnel or industrial relations departments and putting more responsibility for this area on to line managers.

The intention behind both moves has been to improve the implementation of industrial relations policies. The elements of the policies are rarely under debate; though many line managers would argue that there could still be a lot more emphasis on efficiency and control. The problems arise in the way the various elements of the policy fit together and the extent to which the industrial relations policy contributes to the total success of the organisation. If the espoused industrial relations policy does not contribute in that way it will fail to become part of the operational policy. That will mean that in general line management, who tend to follow the operational policy, will ignore it. In turn, that will mean that relationships with staff, which are determined by the way managers treat their subordinates, will not be affected by the written-down policies which were intended to define that relationship.

There may be stages of sophistication in industrial relations policies which apparently develop through a cycle. Many organisations still regard all manpower issues as a nuisance – detailed and annoying intrusions that have to be faced once the important decisions have been made and management is trying to implement those decisions. Many companies now, however, have realised that industrial relations are important in a positive sense rather than just negatively, in the problems they can create. The managers in those organisations have tended to elevate industrial relations as a specialism in its own right, with special departments of experts creating detailed and progressive espoused industrial relations policies. The third stage is evident in some of our bigger and more sophisticated companies. They are moving away from detailed, clearly written policy documents as a focus of their activities and towards a more generalised understanding amongst senior executives of the need to integrate man management into all other aspects of the business.

Activity

Which stage is your organisation at? Take a few minutes to answer the following questions.

1 Is the picture I have drawn in this chapter too futuristic?
2 Do many organisations realise the importance of manpower and the role of good industrial relations? Does your organisation?
3 Can you identify the key elements of your organisation's operational policy and its effect on industrial relations?

Further reading

In this book I have deliberately kept references to other written work to an absolute minimum. The books listed below will help you to follow up particular subjects in more detail.

There is another book in the Breakthrough series which can usefully be read alongside this one:

Roger Oldcorn, *Management: A Fresh Approach*, Pan Breakthrough, 1982.

Industrial relations books that you might find interesting, and that should be easily available from any bookshop, including the following.

General

ACAS, *Industrial Relations Handbook*, HMSO, 1980.
W. Brown, *The Changing Contours of British Industrial Relations*, Blackwell, 1981.
H. A. Clegg, *The Changing System of Industrial Relations In Great Britain*, Blackwell, 1979.
J. Purcell, *Good Industrial Relations*, Macmillan, 1981.

On the management of industrial relations

K. Hawkins, *The Management of Industrial Relations*, Penguin, 1978.
K. Hawkins, *A Handbook of Industrial Relations Practice*, Kogan Page, 1979.
M. Marchington, *Managing Industrial Relations*.

On trade unions

H. Pelling, *A History of British Trade Unionism*, Macmillan, 1976.
K. Coates and A. Topham, *Trade Unions in Britain*, Spokesman, 1982.

On the state in industrial relations

C. Crouch, *The Politics of Industrial Relations*, Fontana, 1979.
K. W. Wedderburn, *The Worker and the Law*, Penguin, 1971.

On workplace industrial relations

T. Nichols, *Living with Capitalism*, Routledge, 1977.
E. Batstone *et al.*, *Shop Stewards in Action*, Blackwell, 1977.
A. Fox, *Man Mismanagement*, Hutchinson, 1974.

There are further references in each of these books, if you want to continue your studies in these subjects.

You should not overlook the often free publications by official bodies: ACAS codes of practice, Department of Employment guides to legislation and so on. You can get the address of each from the telephone book.

Regular publications include the invaluable *Department of Employment Gazette*, *Industrial Relations Review and Report*, *Incomes Data Services*, and *Personnel Management*. All four journals should be available in a good library.

You can learn a lot about industrial relations by reading the newspapers; but you must remember that they have their own values too. The best place to read about industrial relations in the press is the labour column of the *Financial Times* (and it is not difficult to read), but all newspapers include industrial relations stories.

Glossary of terms

action (industrial action) Any deviation from normal working practice taken by an individual or a group collectively in pursuit of an objective on which they are in conflict with management.

arbitration The process of resolving disputes by reference to the decision of a third party.

ban overtime/overtime ban A particular type of industrial action where employees refuse to work outside their normal contractual working hours.

blacking Type of industrial action which takes the form of a boycott, i.e. refusing to handle or work with particular items or people. Often used by workers in sympathy with striking employees whereby goods from the strikebound site will not be handled by work-people in other organisations.

blue-collar workers Workers employed in manual work.

branch A local organisation of a trade union, geographically or organisation-based.

breakdown The point at which the parties in negotiation cannot reach agreement and discussions can no longer continue.

check-off System whereby the employer deducts union subscriptions from wages on behalf of the union.

claim A term applied to the proposal put forward by the employees at the beginning of a negotiation.

clock on/clock off 'Clock on' describes the stamping of a time card by employees at the clocking-on machine when they start work. They will also have to clock off at the end of their work period.

closed shop An agreement between an employer and trade union (or a number of trades unions) that all employees become or remain members of the union(s).

code of practice Document issued by the government or a government agency to provide guidance on a specified topic. It can be quoted in legal cases.

collective agreement An agreement reached between management and trade union(s) which covers a particular work group. Normally a collective agreement is specifically applied to a work group (often referred to as a bargaining unit) and is unlikely to affect other members of the union(s).

collective bargaining The process through which management representatives and union representatives jointly make collective agreements. Collective bargaining is applied to those negotiations specifically concerned with the changing of terms and conditions of employment.

conciliation The process of resolving disputes by involving a third party who does not make a decision but tries to aid the process of reaching agreement.

contract of employment The fundamental legal relationship between employer and employee, governing what an employee must do and what he must receive. Some of the actual details concerning the job will be stated in the written terms and conditions of employment, which is not the contract of employment, merely evidence of it.

convenor The senior shop steward within an organisation elected by the shop stewards. This person normally acts as the leader of the union representatives and speaks on their behalf in meetings with management.

custom and practice Unwritten understandings or beliefs which have grown up within a workplace over a period of time and which have come to be accepted as part of the rules of that workplace.

demarcation An insistence that only particular workers are allowed to do particular tasks.

differential Differences between rates of pay for individuals or groups for jobs (including additional payments which may be made for length of service, responsibility, etc.). They can be formally agreed or established in a piecemeal fashion.

disciplinary procedure The method, often agreed between management and employees or their union(s), for dealing with shortcomings in employees' conduct and behaviour.

dismissal The ending of an employee's employment with an organisation by the employer.

dispute An unresolved issue between employees and their

employer. 'Disputes procedure' is the method agreed by employers and employees which they will follow in order to resolve the dispute.

district official The first level of full-time union official (paid by the union) with responsibility for the membership within a particular geographical locality.

elected representatives Those people who through a method of voting have been given the job of acting on behalf of a group of employees. Often referred to as shop stewards.

employee relations A general term to describe the way that people at work behave and relate to each other and the organisation for which they work. Often used in place of 'industrial relations', which may give an impression of a manufacturing environment or conflict-based relationships.

employers' association An organisation of employers in the same industry. Often an association will negotiate on behalf of the employers with the trade unions representing the employees of the member organisations and therefore establish national agreements. The associations offer other services to the member organisations, such as business advice, information and training.

flexibility/job flexibility Job flexibility refers to the relaxing of the barriers between jobs, allowing employees to do other jobs as well. Often agreement for flexibility has to be negotiated and it is not a simple case of telling an employee that they will now do something else in order to perform effectively.

flexitime An arrangement where individual employees can choose the times at which they start and finish work between certain stated hours. Normally there will be a core time where everyone is expected to be present, and normally the minimum number of hours to be worked within a period of four weeks will also be stated.

genuine occupational qualification Reasons such as authenticity or decency which are allowed by law to exempt the employer from the sex and race discrimination legislation.

grievance A complaint or problem raised formally by an employee.

grievance procedure A formal process, often agreed between management and employees or their union(s) for resolving grievances.

gross misconduct Certain actions in breach of company rules which are considered to be so unreasonable that they can lead to summary (instant) dismissal.

guarantee payments Statutory payments which the employer must make to workers laid off or on short time.

health and safety representative A person elected to help monitor health and safety practices and employees' welfare and to ensure that the workplace is as safe and healthy as can be reasonably expected.

induction training The training associated with introducing new employees to their place of work and to their job.

industrial relations A very broad term describing the relationship between employees, working groups and their representing organisations, on the one hand, and managers, employers and their representing organisations on the other.

joint regulation There have to be rules about how organisations work if they are to function at all. Sometimes management establishes these rules independently. But there are issues, particularly those which directly affect everyone in an organisation, on which rules are agreed between management and the workforce or, more normally, their representatives. This process is called joint regulation.

labour costs Whenever work is being done, and whatever the job, the actual cost of doing the work will include an element of the cost of the person/people doing the work. This cost element is a proportion, related to the time spent on that job, of the total cost of employing that person/people. The total labour costs are the sum of those costs which an employer pays, both voluntary and statutory, to all the employees.

lay-off Temporary suspension of the contract of employment; usually because no work is available.

line management Refers to managers who are responsible for those parts of a company directly involved in providing the product or service which it sells (e.g. production, sales). Line departments are the opposite of 'staff' functions, like personnel and accounts, which provide a support service.

local level Activities at a particular work site.

member The name given to a person who has joined a union.

national official A full-time official employed by the union, usually based at head office, working through the district official. They usually have trade or industry responsibility, or a geographical responsibility, or a mixture of both.

negotiation The process whereby elected or nominated representatives for different groups discuss an issue in order to achieve a satisfactory solution for the parties concerned.

negotiating rights When management has recognised a representing body, often a union, to negotiate on behalf of the people it represents, that representing body is said to have achieved negotiating rights.

participation Describes the enormous variety of methods, structures and activities through which employees are involved in the decision-making processes of the organisation which employs them.

personnel department A specialist department concerned with the people employed in an organisation and policies and practices which regulate employment.

personnel manager/officer A person concerned with people at work and their relationships within an organisation, who provides a specialist service to others.

picketing The action of employees on strike, who gather outside their place of work peacefully to persuade others to join them.

probationary period A fixed time (which will vary between organisations) during which a new employee will have to achieve a satisfactory work standard and only after which permanent employment commences.

procedures Established methods for dealing with workplace issues like grievances and discipline.

production area The part of an organisation where products are manufactured.

production manager The person in charge of the production department, buildings, plant, material and manpower and the amount of production from these resources.

productivity A measure of efficiency. It takes account of various factors, most importantly the time taken to produce x number of products. Greater efficiency is achieved if more products can be produced in a shorter amount of time (assuming costs remain relatively stable). Hence, productivity is improved.

recognition An acceptance by management that a trade union or other representing body has been given the right to represent a group of employees on specific issues in discussions with management.

redundancy Situations where a worker or workers are no longer required by an organisation, because either their continued employment or their particular skills are surplus to requirements.

rules Policies, procedures and practices which regulate employment. Often they have been established through collective bargaining.

shop floor A workplace or department, usually implying a production department and associated departments, e.g. stores or transport.

shop steward An elected trade union representative, representing a group of trade union members in a section of a workplace/department.

staff Usually refers to non-manual employees. In single-status organisations, i.e. those organisations which do not distinguish between manual and non-manual employees, it is applied to all employees. Can also be used to distinguish those people not involved in 'line functions'.

staff representative Often used to describe the union representatives for non-manual employees and therefore equivalent to 'shop steward'. However, it is also applied to representatives on consultative committees in non-union workplaces.

strike The stoppage of work by employees as a collective breach of their contracts of employment, but with the intention of returning to work at a later date.

supervisor A manager directly responsible for members of a specific work group.

terms and conditions What is expected of an employee and what an employee can expect for working for an organisation, i.e. basic working hours, basic payment rates, holidays, overtime, shifts, etc.

trade union An association of people in employment who have joined together to maintain or improve their working lives. A trade union will usually represent a certain type of employee. The usual distinctions are trade unions representing craft workers, trade unions representing manual workers of a general nature and trade unions representing white-collar workers.

unofficial action Action which is taken by employees and which does not have the formal support of the union as required by its rule-book.

white-collar A term usually applied to non-manual employees.

working practices The actual method and technique, usually specified (though often reinterpreted by the employee), for doing a particular job to achieve the required standard. Working practices may be subject to formal agreement, and therefore changes in practice must also be subject to such agreements.

work measurement The application of techniques designed to establish the time for a qualified worker to carry out a specified job at a defined level of performance. Work measurement is used to define standards of expected work achievements and is often associated with the setting of incentive payments.

works council Some organisations have a works council committee made up of management representatives and employee representatives which discusses matters of common interest. The works council does not generally have negotiating rights.

work to rule A particular type of industrial action whereby the employees work to the strict content of the terms of their contract.

written statement See Part 1 (sections 1 to 11) of the Employment Protection (Consolidation) Act 1978. For most employees an employer is obliged by law to provide a written statement containing at least the main points of the contract of employment, within the first thirteen weeks of the employee starting work.

Index

ACAS 11, 95, 99, 105
adjournments 190
AUEW 69

BALPA 58
bargaining range 169, 176, 208
branch officials 66

CAC 95, 105
CBI 19, 75
changes in work 32
changing law 111
check-off 67
closed shop 146
codes of practice 99
collective agreements in law 108–11
common law 97, 121
confederations 72
Conservative Party 19, 87, 89
consultation 158
contract of employment 18, 116
control 142, 200
conventions 164
coordination 142

definition of IR 13
demand 171
departmental differences 41
Department of Employment 96
disciplinary procedures 155
discrimination 122

EETPU 69
efficiency 203
election of officials 70
employee representatives (*see also*
    shop stewards) 60–5
employers' associations 47–50
espoused policies 196

federations 72
flexibility of labour 204–6
full-time officials 69

general secretaries 69
golden formula 107
grievance procedures 152

health and safety 98, 126–32

implied terms 118
incomes policies 83–7
industrial sector 28
industrial tribunals 98
inflation rates 82
informal arrangements 148, 159

Labour Party 54, 74, 82, 87
line managers 42

management controls 158
management
    as employees 51
    definition 35
    differences within 39
    hierarchy 43–7
    objectives 37
maternity rights 124–6
MSC 96
multi-unionism 59, 199

NEDO 96

negotiating, definition 162
new technology 32, 195
non-union companies 159
NUS 69

occupational structure 31
operational policies 197
opinions 12
owners 35

performance 194
picketing 108
policies 196
political connections 87
power in negotiations 167
preparation 176
private sector 29
procedures 148
public sector 29

recruitment and selection law 114
redundancy 137
resistance points 174
right to strike 106
Royal Commission on Unions and
    Employers' Associations 65
rules 143

self-employment 16, 200
simplicity in IR 198
size of workplace 30

shop stewards 62–4
stability 201
staff managers 42
state
    as economic manager 81
    as employer 77
    as IR specialist 95
    as law-giver 90
statue law 97
strikes 24–6

tactics in negotiations 188
targets in negotiations 171
team roles 179
termination of employment 132
TGWU 62
time off 123
trade unions 54–75
trade union recognition 102, 145
TUC 11, 19, 73

unfair dismissal 133–7

variety of workplaces 28, 139
voluntarism 91, 100

wages councils 94, 117
Whitley Committee 79
work as a central activity 21
written satatement of terms and
    conditions 118

Reference, language and information

☐	**A Guide to Insurance**	Margaret Allen	£1.95p
☐	**The Story of Language**	C. L. Barber	£1.95p
☐	**North-South**	Brandt Commission	£2.50p
☐	**Test Your IQ**	Butler and Pirie	£1.25p
☐	**Writing English**	D. J. Collinson	£1.50p
☐	**Manifesto**	Francis Cripps et al	£1.95p
☐	**Buying and Selling a House or Flat**	Marjorie Giles	£1.75p
☐	**Save It! The Energy Consumer's Handbook**	Hammond, Newport and Russell	£1.25p
☐	**Mathematics for the Million**	L. Hogben	£1.95p
☐	**Dictionary of Famous Quotations**	Robin Hyman	£2.95p
☐	**Militant Islam**	Godfrey Jansen	£1.50p
☐	**The State of the World Atlas**	Michael Kidron and Ronald Segal	£6.95p
☐	**The War Atlas**	Michael Kidron and Dan Smith	£5.95p
☐	**Practical Statistics**	R. Langley	£1.95p
☐	**How to Study**	H. Maddox	£1.75p
☐	**Your Guide to the Law**	ed. Michael Molyneux	£3.95p
☐	**Common Security**	Palme Commission	£1.95p
☐	**The Modern Crossword Dictionary**	Norman Pulsford	£2.95p
☐	**A Guide to Saving and Investment**	James Rowlatt	£2.50p
☐	**Career Choice**	Audrey Segal	£2.95p
☐	**Logic and its Limits**	Patrick Shaw	£2.95p
☐	**Names for Boys and Girls**	L. Sleigh and C. Johnson	£1.75p
☐	**Straight and Crooked Thinking**	R. H. Thouless	£1.95p
☐	**The Best English**	G. H. Vallins	80p
☐	**First Clue: The A-Z of Finding Out**	Robert Walker	£2.50p
☐	**Money Matters**	Harriet Wilson	£1.25p
☐	**Dictionary of Earth Sciences**		£2.95p
☐	**Dictionary of Economics and Commerce**		£1.50p
☐	**Dictionary of Life Sciences**		£2.95p
☐	**Dictionary of Physical Sciences**		£2.95p
☐	**Harrap's New Pocket French and English Dictionary**		£2.50p
☐	**The Limits to Growth**		£2.50p

Management

☐	**Introducing Management**	Christopher, McDonald and Wills	£1.95p
☐	**The Effective Executive**	} Peter Drucker	£1.75p
☐	**Management**		£3.50p
☐	**Under New Management**	Tony Eccles	£2.95p
☐	**How to Double Your Profits**	John Fenton	£3.50p
☐	**Inside Business Law**	} David Field	£2.95p
☐	**Inside Employment Law**		£2.50p
☐	**How to Win Customers**	Heinz Goldmann	£2.95p
☐	**Gods of Management**	Charles Handy	£1.25p
☐	**The Black Economy**	Arnold Heertje *et al.*	£1.95p
☐	**Managing People at Work**	John Hunt	£2.50p
☐	**Investment Appraisal for Managers**	Graham Mott	£1.95p
☐	**Managing With Computers**	Terry Rowan	£2.95p
☐	**Guide to Saving and Investment**	James Rowlatt	£2.50p
☐	**Reality of Management**	} Rosemary Stewart	£1.75p
☐	**Reality of Organisations**		£1.95p
☐	**The Fifth Estate: Britain's Unions in the Modern World**	Robert Taylor	£1.95p
☐	**Bargaining for Results**	John Winkler	£1.95p
☐	**Dictionary of Economics and Commerce**		£1.50p
☐	**Multilingual Commercial Dictionary**		£3.95p

All these books are available at your local bookshop or newsagent, or can be ordered direct from the publisher. Indicate the number of copies required and fill in the form below   10

....

Name_____
(Block letters please)

Address_____

_____

Send to CS Department, Pan Books Ltd, PO Box 40, Basingstoke, Hants
Please enclose remittance to the value of the cover price plus:
35p for the first book plus 15p per copy for each additional book ordered
to a maximum charge of £1.25 to cover postage and packing
Applicable only in the UK

While every effort is made to keep prices low, it is sometimes
necessary to increase prices at short notice. Pan Books reserve
the right to show on covers and charge new retail prices which
may differ from those advertised in the text or elsewhere